GHANA:
DIARY OF A SON'S
SANKOFA RETURN

(BECOMING KWEKU)

WILLIE (KWEKU) SINGLETON

Order this book online at www.trafford.com
or email orders@trafford.com

Most Trafford titles are also available at major online book retailers.

Print information available on the last page.

ISBN: 978-1-4269-0635-0 (sc)
ISBN: 978-1-4907-5982-1 (hc)
ISBN: 978-1-4269-0636-7 (e)

Library of Congress Control Number: 2015904925

Trafford rev. 05/11/2015

 www.trafford.com

North America & international
toll-free: 1 888 232 4444 (USA & Canada)
fax: 812 355 4082

AUTHOR'S NOTES

SANKOFA
(Return and take it)

Since a visit to Ghana was my first opportunity to visit a country in Africa, Ghana became symbolic of my unknown past. Without knowing the African country, in which my ancestors originated, I (sans bias) tend to identify with all the African countries. I think of me as a Pan African. Despite Thomas Wolfe's words, "you can't go home again", I wanted to go home... I chose to go home... I went home.

From Adinkra symbolisms, the sankofa symbol is represented by a bird reaching back for an egg on its back or sometimes as a fancily designed heart. From the Adinkra, the word means "return and take it". S-a-n-k-o-f-a is a phonetic spelling of the word. The Akan have some alphabet characters not present in the English language. The 'o' is sometimes replaced by a character that resembles a backward 'c' and is pronounced 'aw'.

Sankofa Symbols

The Akan proverb, "Se wo were fi na wosan kofa a yennkyi", translates to English as "It is no taboo to return and fetch it when you forget. You can always undo your mistakes."

This diary narrates my attempts to learn something of what the past once was for those who came before me. My history did not begin with the transatlantic slave trade and certainly not with the Berlin Conference where Africa was carved up and divided among several European countries.

DEDICATION

Through Fred Winston Laryea, I met Nii Amarkai Laryea Fred's alter ego. Nii Amarkai made my trip to Ghana a reality. Unequivocally, the trip was Will-centric. It was all about me. Thanks... without you... supposition... because of you, a real life experience. As I always hoped, my first trip abroad did lead to the African continent. Without your help with the first step (Ghana), perhaps there would have been no Ivory Coast, Nigeria, Kenya, Tanzania, Uganda, or South Africa This book, I sincerely dedicate to Nii Amarkai Laryea and to Atieno whose love, patience, and support make all my endeavors reality.

THE HYPE

Most days in my life
Africa was diminished
By negative hype

I have always believed that there was something special and positive about Africa. So many negative things were expressed about that continent that there had to be much more positives to it. That line of thinking may not sway many polemics, but it was a beginning for me.

Not barbarism … not brutal or raw
The importation of a 'man'
Euphemistically … 'tagged' by the 'law'
"Civilizing the African"

My generation grew up permeated with such overt tenets as: *The slave trade was the best thing that happened to America's blacks. Clothes were put on their naked bodies, and they were fed when taken out of Africa. By and large, the slave masters were kind benevolent people and were loved by their slaves. Africa, and consequently Africans, have never contributed anything to world culture. In addition to this, all eyes could see that a white, Tarzan, reigned as the* <u>unchallenged</u> *and* <u>undisputed</u> *king of the dark continent.*

There was more of that falderal, but I trust that you understand the bent. Childhood pals will tell you that I often questioned much of this. At an early age, I doubted that all Africans were primitives. Early on, I read of civilizations in ancient Mali and Ghana. Why was Egypt portrayed so differently, i.e. *much more positive* when compared to the other African countries? Was Egypt thought African? Did it have any link to black Africa? Were all of Egypt's accomplishments from non African countries who had conquered it?

How many times have I seen and heard individuals from different parts of Africa asked... do you speak African. Those asking the question were black and white. As of today, I have yet to see/hear individuals from different parts of Europe asked... do you speak European... nor have I heard it asked of people from any other continent. Perhaps I missed it.

In one of my classes, I even gave a talk suggesting that if Jesus Christ were a Falasha or an original Jew, he may have been of African descent. My teacher and my classmates had extreme difficulty with that notion. More current to later times, I wondered where the heroic black cowboys and other black heroes were. Never were they shown on the movie screen and seldom mentioned in the history books. Until recently, any screen depiction of an African (from any country) was a caricature.

The whites in my *multicultural school* even called a strike and did not attend classes for close to two months. They didn't want any black (sons/daughters of Africa) students attending... *their* school.

Classmates... black and white
had hopes of seeing Europe
I chose Africa

On graduating from high school, classmates, happily and eagerly, verbally expressed plans to one day visit the well publicized European capitals, e.g. London, Paris, Rome, Athens, etc. On desiring to see those capitals, there was a racial intersection. Many blacks also longed to see those same places. For me, any trip abroad, whenever and however unlikely at that time, had to lead to some country in Africa. My thoughts were unwavering.

When I went to the corporate world, the black population increased from 3 to 4 (a slight over exaggeration). In the company lunch room, a white cashier, directing her comment toward black employees, was heard to say *"jungle bunnies"*. She vehemently denied making the statement. In the lounge area, an oriental whispered... "niggers". He, just as vehemently, denied making such a statement. No one pushed the matter... probably because he was suspected to be a karate master (loosen up and smile a bit... but just a bit).

One of my best friends was never able to convince his father that not all of Africa was dense jungle. A good black member of a Lutheran church once told me that black people had no culture at all. That pronouncement was traumatic to me and helped to serve as a catalyst motivating me to learn more about African culture... in my view... my culture.

In a way, I compare the trauma of people forcefully taken from the African continent to *the psychological chaos that manifests itself when children are unwillingly taken away from one or both parents.* A child living apart from one parent may get bombarded with disparaging comments about the missing parent. The commenter may be a parent, relative, or outsider. Eventually the child may begin to believe and echo the comments he/she has been bombarded with.

Perhaps the impact of the comments may cause the child to dislike the missing parent. Despite all that, others are able to 'shake it off' and not believe the negative hype. In fact, love for the absent parent may grow. My love for Africa grew. True to that thought, the time quickly came when many of my thoughts turned to wanting to see my parents, i.e. Africa, from whom I had been so long separated. I have no idea of the specific African country where my ancestors originated. Consequently, I cling to all of Africa.

Quite truthfully, as each year passed, I found myself procrastinating too often and did little or nothing to ensure that I would see some part of Africa. On one occasion, a friend told me about a group planning a trip to Sierra Leone. I agreed to go, but the trip never materialized. It may have been canceled.

THE DOOR OPENS

A few years later, I was affably nudged toward Africa, and the outcome of that nudge is what this diary is about. This writing is a partial account of my three and one-half week stay in Ghana, West Africa during the month of August 1992.

One born in Ghana
One of African descent
Two became good friends

Fred Laryea, who I met at work, seemed to be a nice enough person. At first, I didn't know much about him other than he was African... For that matter, despite many opposing views, so am I. The first few times that I saw him, he was most often in the presence of Asians or whites.

That was true whether it was at lunch or on break. I don't know that I consciously, or otherwise, responded to that, but I did notice it. Perhaps some negative vibes did exude... unconsciously that is. If so, some of you may think of me as racist for that. Admittedly, I am somewhat suspect when I see a brother or a sister so often outside *the black wing. Putting it another way, he was never in the company of anyone black. Gather up all your data, and* we can debate this if you wish... Should we agree to do so, let's do it at a later date. At this time, I am not in a *debating frame of mind.*

Fred stopped me one day, and although unsolicited, he explained to me why he was so often in the presence of that company. If memory serves me accurately, it seems that he and the others had started work, with the company, at approximately the same time. It also seems that those comrades had made efforts to go their separate ways.

Some wanted to eat lunch *with their own*. At his appearance, others made remarks such as *"here comes the African monkey out of his tree"*. He was made to feel that he was tagging along. You and Fred can discuss those particulars. In any event, Fred and I became *lunch buddies*... and more importantly... friends.

Fred had invited another 'brother', David Miller, to go home with him to Ghana. Later the invitation was extended to me. At first, I thought he was *kidding around*... I thought the invitation was jest. He assured me that the invitation was genuine. The door had been opened.

As much as I dislike flying, the invitation was one that I could not refuse. It was an opportunity that I did not want to miss. Many times, I had wondered about the continent that was the birth place of ancestors... without whom my existence would not be.

The invitation had been offered in early June. Not until I began to get inoculated and actually bought my ticket did I begin to realize that I was very serious about this trip. The flight was scheduled for August 1, 1992... destination... Accra, Ghana.

Approximately 3 days prior to the departure date, I began to feel exuberant and became more eager and excited about seeing a part of West Africa.

Thursday, July 30 - I had lunch with the *old work gang, i.e.* Carolyn Hill, Marge Newsome, Dorian Walden and Doris Robinson. Carolyn's daughter had recently died. After the funeral, Doris had suggested that we take Carolyn out to lunch upon her return to work. Dorian had suggested that Doris take responsibility for arranging the lunch. We all knew that Doris' prior behavior had manifested a style that was somewhat remiss when responding to plans that had been made.

Not to be outdone, Doris took care of business... arranging rides and telling us what time to meet at the Red Lobster Inn in Piscataway, New Jersey. I thought the *get together* was nice enough although much of the conversation shifted toward 'lady talk'. Each of them (I think) promised to pray that I would have a safe flight to and from Ghana. After lunch, we all embraced warmly, and they wished me all the best.

Friday, July 31 - Fred Laryea, the brother, who opened the door resulting in my opportunity to see Ghana, and I are co-workers. He is a developer, and I am a product tester. Today his uncle, Samuel Ekuban, visited the work place, and I had the opportunity to meet him. To me, he has a striking resemblance to my younger brother Ivory. Without a doubt, they certainly do 'flavor'... you know... unmistakably... very black African. The name that Mr. Ekuban prefers is Nana *Sam*. In the Fanti language, *Nana* translates as *Chief* in English.

Although I didn't meet her, he told me that his wife's name is *Regina*, and she prefers to be called *Rex*. I began to wonder about the significance of names such as *Fred, Sam and Rex*. My suspicions were that they had little or nothing to do with Ghanaian names. Sam and Rex were visiting Fred in Paterson, New Jersey. We were to leave them in the U. S. They would return to Accra at a later date while we would still be there.

I asked Fred if his uncle's visit at work was *to check me out*. It would be at the home of the Ekuban's where we would reside while in Ghana. Fred's answer was No... I 'sup-POSE' that I believe him... That warrants a smile.

Cathy Goodwater (I think her married name is Jackson) expressed dismay that I did not tell her that I was going to Accra. I told her that not to do so was typically me. She agreed that I was 'private'. Her concern was that I would leave without allowing her the opportunity (through me) to purchase goods from Ghana.

I told her that I would work late that night, and she could bring money for her purchases before I left. Again she agreed. I must admit that I was somewhat surprised when she did return later that night... with fifty dollars. She wanted a size 12 woman's dress, a man's garb for her husband... (xtra large, waist 36), a walking cane (dark grain) and a trinket, or something that I could choose for her young daughter Tia.

Valerie, Brenda, Robin, Theresa and Migdalia all stopped by my office to wish me a great trip. Yesterday, Geri, whose husband is from Gambia, assured me that I would have a great time. "Imagine" she said,... "seeing someone just like you... in charge". Maurice Cooper wished me well and seemed to echo Geri's sentiments. David Miller, who could not go on the trip, was equally gracious.

Rochelle Swerchek, Shu Young, Jack Chao, and Joe Lewis made positive references to the trip.

Saturday, August 1 - The young African, Wes, said emphatically... "Dad, you know how you are with names. In Africa, when you are not sure of names... KEEP YOUR MOUTH CLOSED!". This lack of confidence began, I think, when I referred to one of his friends as *Floppo*. Actually the friend was called *Frito*. Sometimes it seems that I can still hear the laughter, from Wes and his friends, directed at my faux pas.

I spent a few hours, at stores, looking for larger suitcases. Erroneously, I thought that Fred needed/wanted to pack a few of his things in my bags. Packing took longer than I thought. Fred was told that I would meet him at Newark Airport at 6:00 p.m. I almost left the house with my medicine, toiletries and other things remaining on my dresser. Wes stopped me adding that I should be very thankful that he was there. Of course, he was right. I had to agree.

NEWARK TO LONDON

(FIRST LEG)

When I arrived at the airport, I needed a cart to get my baggage to the check-in spot. I wrenched my back on the escalator when the cart almost tipped over. I tried to balance the cart and the baggage. That was not a good move. I tried to go directly to the gate, but I had to go back to check my bags.

Near the baggage check-in area, I saw Fred pacing frantically. When he saw me, he barked something about his having given up on me. Additionally he told me that he had called my home, and Wes told him that I had left about 30 minutes earlier. It was easy to determine that he was miffed, bothered, angry, and whatever else. Sarcastically, he continued "usually you are so reliable".

There was not much response from me. The bag that I had hoped to carry on was too heavy. Consequently, I had to check it. I forgot that my camcorder and books, to be read on the flight, were in that bag. It was too late to get them back. I would have to deal with the mini crisis.

Fred had to rub it in because there was no way that I could guarantee that the camera would not be damaged. Since the British had colonized Ghana as well as the USA, I enjoyed referring to Fred as 'the Brit'. The *Brit*, Fred, called my carelessness... naiveté. After moments of verbal jabs, Fred calmed down.

Then it was my turn.

I told Fred that I had refused to comment while he was angry. It would have been his anger against my anger. The results, I stated emphatically, would have meant my *kicking his behind*. We both had a big laugh as we proceeded toward the gate.

When I went through the gate, the alarm went off. I had keys and other things in my pockets. After removing them, everything seemed o.k. That buoyant feeling that I had earlier was returning. I felt so ebullient... so very exuberant... that I had no misgivings about flying which is obviously not one of my favorite pastimes.

Earlier that euphoria was dampened somewhat when I went to buy suitcases. When I placed the suitcases on the counter, the cashier had to go through all the pockets on the suitcases to determine whether or not I had stored (that's a euphemism for stolen) articles in the pockets. Granted that may have been her job, but my experiences suggested that rule would not be followed across the board.

Needless to say, I verbally and strongly objected. Who was it who said, "show me a black man in America who does not suffer from symptoms of paranoia, and I will show you a sick man".

For some reason, the incident caused me to think about the *Public Enemy Rap Song*, i.e. *Don't Believe the Hype. HEY!* Enough of America... let's get to the Motherland.

I never thought of myself as musical, but now it seems that events are suggesting musical numbers to me. In my head, I could hear the Ohio Players performing *'I Want to Be Free'* as I thought: I'm going home... British Airways... Flight BA0184 on a Boeing 747. Because I checked in late, Fred and I were not assigned adjoining seats. Fred spoke to a flight attendant about *seat manipulation*. An Indian woman seated next to Fred wanted to sit next to her friend. She moved. I took her seat, and the other person took my seat.

Sitting on Fred's other side was a Jewish man. I was not introduced to him, but Fred called him... Abie, and he responded. He and Fred seemed to hit it off well. They talked a lot. Now there is another logistics problem. We had to move again... the three of us Fred, Abie, and me.

Room had to be made for three other passengers. I still don't understand the logic of that move. It seems that the other three could have moved to the area where we were requested to move. Perhaps there were more than three in their party... I don't know.

Abie was adamant in his refusal to move. He mentioned something about his seat being kosher. Don't ask me what that means. I don't have the slightest idea. I moved, but Fred remained with Abie. Maybe Fred was protecting *Abie's Rights*. You know... as in Fred thinking... *"What's the matter Abie? WE got problems"*... I don't know.

Finally the two of them joined me. We were scheduled to leave at 7:40p.m. The plane took off about 8:00p.m. bound for Heathrow Airport in London, England... the first leg of the trip. The flight to London was to be seven and one half hours.

True to my druthers
my trip abroad was leading
to THE CONTINENT

When we were airborne, Fred asked... "where is your passport"? I told him that I left it in the bag that I checked thinking that the bag would be with me. He realized that I was putting him on and countered with, "don't B.S. me"... only he didn't say B-S.

Fred wanted to know the day of the week on which I was born and the political climate at that time. Those factors, according to him, help in naming a child born to his tribe... Ga. I hated to tell him that I did not know any of that data. In a stentorian voice, he then bellowed his tribal name... **NII AMARKAI LARYEA**. I think I liked Nii Amarkai... as a person... better than Fred.

We both laughed. I told him that I would have liked it much better had not so many people at work known that we were going to Ghana. A private streak still burns deeply within me. I told him that since we were going to Africa that private bent was tempered somewhat. Fred told me that he took pride in telling others because the destination was Africa, and it made him more happy that I recognized Africa as home.

I think we both felt good about that conversation... I know I did.

James and Bessie had told me that one of their relatives had suggested that they warn me about drinking the water in Ghana. No other specifics were relayed to me. I asked Fred about the water, and he told me that he knew of nothing negative about drinking the water. What he was aware of was that there were times when the water would have a rust like color. When that happens, you let the water run for a short while, and it clears up.

To me, he seemed to describe what had happened to me several times in the USA. Oh well, time will tell. The flight attendant came by serving tea and coffee.

I surmised that the Brits prefer tea. I opted for neither. Instead I asked for soda.

To my dismay, the attendant brought me club soda. Fred, the Brit, told me that I would have to ask for coke, sprite, etc. To the Brits, soda means club soda. I thought about my move from Gary, Indiana to Philadelphia, Pennsylvania. I went into a grocery store, in North Philadelphia's 'village', and asked for pop. The store keeper was befuddled.

By example, I tried to define... *you know... coke, strawberry, 7-up.* "Oh!"... the merchant replied "you mean soda". That use of soda was then added to my vocabulary. 'Pop' was the name used in Gary, Indiana and also in many southern cities.

Fred seemed to do a lot of sleeping on the plane. I did less. After watching the movie 'Mambo Kings', I finally dozed a bit. Most of the flight was great, but I tensed up with the slightest turbulence. Fred would chuckle and ask if I were O.K. I was O.K.

I don't think my uneasiness with flying manifested itself as Fred thought it would. I am not quite sure what he expected... perhaps continual screaming. Abie and Fred had an on-going conversation. Fred asked Abie, why he, an Orthodox Jew, was flying on Saturday. I heard Abie st_ st_ stutter something... unintelligible, and I chuckled to myself.

Sunday, August 2 - In flight, Saturday, August 1 had become Sunday, August 2. I remember the pilot saying that the altitude would be 33,000 feet and the speed 560 miles per hour. At 1:40 a.m., Eastern Daylight Saving Time, we landed at Heathrow Airport. In London, the time was 5:40 a.m. It was truly *a foggy day in London town.* It was also cool, and my lightweight white jacket felt very comfortable.

Will (one of African descent) Landing at
Heathrow Airport in London

Fred was to meet an uncle there. He wasn't sure at which airport the meeting was to take place. Additionally, he had left his uncle's phone number home in Paterson, New Jersey... Now it was my turn to needle him.

You people can't do anything correctly... I scolded him. I told him that I could have reminded him what to do, but I wanted to give 'a backward person' an opportunity to demonstrate that he was becoming more responsible. Fred's expression seemed to display a failed attempt at a smile.

So I am told, most functions in London revolve around some kind of queue. So it was to be this day. We had to queue up to get our passports checked and to get free tickets for our ride to Gatwick Airport from where we would depart for Accra, Ghana.

HEATHROW TO GATWICK

Fred Laryea (one born in Ghana) to the Speedlink

We left for the Gatwick Airport via the Speedlink Bus. The Speedlink seems to run between the Heathrow Airport and the Gatwick Airport. En route, Fred pointed out that the steering wheels on cars were built on the right hand side of the cars, and the cars drove on the left hand side of the road. That much... I knew.

On the bus, Fred and another African recognized each other as fellow Ghanaians. I don't know what motivated the other man's conclusion, but Fred saw a tribal mark, under the man's right eye, that he recognized. Fred identified a horizontal cut approximately one inch below the eye and concluded that the man was a member of Ghana's Fanti tribe.

My teacher (Fred) further explained that his own tribe (Ga) often had two cuts one on each side. It could be on the corners of the lips or eyes. Tribal marks were more prevalent in Northern Ghana (Dagomba and Frafrah tribes). Their aggressive cuts were referred to as the 'Lion'.

Cuts were four concentric circles from the forehead around the eyebrow and cheek. Additionally there was a slash from the bridge of the nose down to the cheekbone. The cuts were done when the recipients were babies. A concoction that was to ward off evil spirits was used. In Ghana, tribal marks, like female circumcision, are now done less frequently.

The Speedlink driver was black. He announced that they would provide snacks and soft drinks. I was surprised that this would be *provided* on a relatively short trek. The vendor, who was also black, stopped at each seat asking "who wants snacks or drinks".

There were so many refusals that I concluded *providing does not equate to gratis*. Other passengers had also thought that the snacks were free until the vendor asked for fifty pence. That was approximately 96 cents. $1.92 was equal to one pound which was equal to 100 pence.

When the vendor reached our seats, Fred said to him "you look like a Nigerian". Later Fred would tell me that it was more that he sounded like a Nigerian than he looked like a Nigerian. In any event, the vendor said only "I'm afraid not"... as he moved on.

Fred's second guess was that he may have been Jamaican. My guess, that he was South African, could not have been any worse than Fred's. Why was that my guess? Well, to me, he resembled Hugh Masekela the South African musician.

We never did find out which, if either, of us was correct. Most of the cars that we passed seemed to be small in size... you know economy cars. As we neared our stop, we saw an unattended plane in the

Ghana Airline fleet. The emblem on the plane was red, gold and green with a black star in the middle inside the gold area. This was symbolic of the Ghanaian flag.

Although we were not flying Ghana Airlines, I had never seen a commercial plane that I knew to be owned by a black individual or country. This one was owned by an African nation... Ghana. The ride from Heathrow to Gatwick must have taken 30 to 40 minutes. When we got off the bus, Fred called his wife to get his uncle's phone number. The number that she gave him was incorrect, so he had to call her again. When Fred called his uncle's home, his uncle was not

A decal of the Ghana flag

there. The person answering the phone told Fred that his uncle had gone to Heathrow Airport, but they would give him the message and have him call Fred at the pay phone Fred was using.

He did call, and they both lamented at having gotten their wires crossed. Fred wanted to get a taxi and go to Middlesex where his uncle lived. His uncle advised him against that, and they made plans to meet on our return from Ghana.

A point of interest, I thought, was that the British refer to bathrooms as showers and the W.C. on the door refers to water closet. I did see *Gentlemen* written on a water closet. I saw no designation for the ladies.

Fred had suggested that we go to downtown London... you know Buckingham Palace and some other places. When we got squared away, there were only four hours left until flight time. From the airport, it would take about one and one half hours to get down town. That would mean that 3 hours would be shot on travel alone. We had considered renting a car, but we would not have enough time for the trip.

There was still time on our hands. At Gatwick, there is a free train between terminals. We were in the North Terminal and trained to the South Terminal. In the South Terminal, there seemed to be much more activity going on. There were stores, restaurants, etc. We sat down in a restaurant, ate a chicken order, and walked around until it was time to board for Ghana.

I tasted London water and concluded that the taste was awful. Fred agreed. By now, I am sure that you have surmised that I am *not big* on flying. One thing that I have always said is that I wanted my first trip abroad to lead to Africa. It is close to happening. This plane is a DC10 bound for Accra and Abijan the capital of the Ivory Coast.

GATWICK TO ACCRA, GHANA

Again, Fred and I don't have seats together. Fred sat next to Andrew, a white medical student, from Cardiff, Wales. I sat next to Ganu, a Ghanaian, who has been living in Brooklyn. Ganu mentioned that his plane from New York had arrived in London ahead of schedule just as our plane from Newark had. Ganu also mentioned that he liked the window seat. Because of that, I never suggested his changing seats with Fred. Andrew also liked his window seat but seemed amenable to moving. No problem, there were two empty middle aisles. Fred and I moved to seats in one of those aisles.

At this point, I was really tired. I had dozed off prior to take off but awakened during the takeoff. To myself, I thought... we are in the air... before dozing off again.

Over the intercom, the pilot mentioned that we would fly over France, Spain, the Pyrenees Mountains, the Mediterranean Sea, North Africa, the Sahara Desert and on to Accra, Ghana. From Accra, some would continue to Abidjan. While in flight, the pilot gave the time in Ghana.

The time he gave would suggest that there was a three hour difference between Eastern Daylight Time and the time in Ghana. Emphatically, Fred denied that the pilot had given that time. To quote him, "HE COULD NOT MAKE SUCH A MISTAKE". Andrew had set his watch by the pilot's information. He mentioned that to Fred, and Fred seemed more receptive.

I told Fred now that Bwana has said what I had earlier said much more authenticity is placed on the pilot's words. There is something to be said for that scenario, but for the moment, I choose to pass.

From Newark to London in a 747, there was a big screen in the front of the cabin. On the DC10, there is a big screen in the front and small monitors on either side near the middle aisle. Our feature was a dog movie called 'Beethoven'. I didn't see much of it. Off and on, I dozed.

On the flight from Newark to London, I saw very few Africans and a host of Europeans. From London to Ghana, it seems that whites are very much in the minority.

Snacks were served. I don't remember which snacks. In many African countries, when an African hands something to someone, in the left hand, it is considered an insult. The recipient is also expected to receive the item in his/her right hand. Fred handed me something in his left hand. Claiming an insult, I refused to accept it. He chuckled, but he did hand the napkin to me in his right hand. Later I would learn that the genesis of that insult may be a traditional assumption that when one goes to the bathroom, wiping requires use of the left hand.

We touched down in Accra at 4 p.m. Eastern Daylight Saving Time. Soon, I would learn that the name of the airport is Kotoka. It is Ghana's only international airport, and it has one terminal. You disembark from the plane as people in the U.S. did about 20 years ago.

One walks down the stairs provided, but instead of being in the terminal, you must wait for a bus that takes you to the terminal. There was a white man directing traffic to the bus. My initial thought was... *uh oh here we go again...* you know what I mean... *the white man in charge syndrome.*

CHECKING IN

That thought had an extremely short life. You have no idea how short. When we entered the terminal, the soldiers were... <u>African</u>; the customs people were... <u>African</u>; the passport people were... <u>African</u>. You name it... _Wall to wall... Africans_.

I saw no white in the airport who appeared to be anyone other than a tourist. First there was an initial passport check. The chaotic part came when we went to claim our luggage. It seemed that not many bags were fed onto the carousel at one time. We waited... and waited... and waited.

Finally we got all the bags. Fred had 8 pieces of luggage, and I had 3 pieces. Now it was time for customs inspection. They are supposed to check through all the luggage. In his 8 pieces of luggage, Fred had so much that he became concerned that the customs people would think that he was in Ghana to sell merchandise.

Should that be determined, he would have to leave a deposit... non returnable should the merchandise be sold.

TO EXIT KOTOKA AIRPORT

In his pocket, Fred's smallest bill was a twenty dollar bill. He asked me for ten dollars. Surreptitiously, he gave the ten to the woman checking our luggage.

Most of the luggage was given a cursory check, but she noticed Fred's camcorder that I had in a shoulder bag. Special notification of the camcorder had to be made. Acting on Fred's suggestion, I also declared my camcorder. I would experience the *bribe* or *quid pro quo* for the remainder of my stay in Ghana. Whatever the request... something is expected in return.

There is one more stop that we had to make at the Customs Excise and Preventive Services Office. Fred took our passports and records into the room. I remained outside the office. He was told that we had to leave a two hundred dollar deposit for each camcorder. On departure, should we be unable to produce the camcorders, our deposits would be forfeited. Of course, Fred came outside to get two hundred dollars from me before completing the registration.

While waiting outside the room, at different times, several men approached me. Each was trying to work a hustle. Most were offering to take the luggage to a taxi outside. Of course, a nice gratuity was expected. They were really active. Some asked... only to return and ask again. My pat answer was *you have to ask the guy inside*. I was referring to Fred.

Fred had prepared me for this. One man came up with a friendly smile and said "give me five dollars". My reply was *I'm sorry*. He smiled and again made the request "give me five dollars". To him, my response was the same. This went on and on.

Another young brother came by *requesting* "give me the English shillings in your pocket". I told him that I didn't have any. Now that I think of it, I did have some English coins that I had picked up at the restaurant in London. He replied "I saw them... give me the English shillings". *No you didn't* I said. Just as quickly, he shot back with "I need money to buy biscuits boss". I told him that I was sorry.

Fred finally came out. By that time, one of his uncles and a few of his nephews had arrived and appeared in the area where Fred exited the room. He was later to say that he identified them to me... I wouldn't bet on that. Things were so hectic.

The hectic atmosphere became even more hectic. Hands were reaching out from all directions trying to control handling our luggage. I thought Fred had identified one fellow as being with us, therefore I allowed him to push the cart holding our luggage. From behind us, Fred yelled "hey Will... do you know what you are doing... are you going to pay him".

After a short struggle, I regained control of the cart. Until that day, I had no notion that *all Africans... perhaps I should say Ghanaians... do indeed look alike.* Please smile... Whew! I was getting into this thing now. *No... No... No* was my response each time a strange hand would vie for control of the cart. There must have been ten hands on the cart... no two belonging to the same person.

Finally we were outside the terminal. Fred's uncle had gone to the parking lot to get his truck. Shortly the strange hands were trying to load the luggage on the truck. *No... No... No* I said. I even told one of Fred's nephews... *No... No... No.* Quizzically he looked at me and calmly replied, "I am Fred's nephew".

The nephews hopped on the back of the truck. Fred and I got in the cab. We were on our way. This was amazing. Fewer than six hours from London to Accra and three hours to get out of Kotoka International Airport. Now we are on our way to North Legon where we will reside while in Ghana.

KOTOKA TO NORTH LEGON

The route will take us via the Kwabenya Road which also leads to the old atomic plant. En route, we saw many many people walking down the road. I am told that this is a common occurrence. My mind shot back to growing up in Gary, Indiana. If we wanted to go anyplace, most often we had to walk.

Fred's uncle is called Colonel (Kennel). His nephews are Adolph and Theophilus. Again my mind wonders... from whence come these names. Oh yes, I should mention that while we were at the airport, on several occasions, Colonel angrily told the hustlers "GO AWAY". They did not go away, but not one, NO not one, said one disrespectful word to him.

As for Fred, he had told me to be strong, and don't give in to the hustlers. Sometimes, he had told me that they run away with the luggage. Who do you think allowed one of them to push a cart with luggage and could be seen shelling out a few dollars? You are most certainly correct... it was not me.

Later I asked whether or not they were hustlers or simply in need. Fred suggested that many of them were really in need. I wish I had known. Without a doubt, I would have kicked in a few dollars.

Upon arriving at the house, Colonel led us in prayer giving thanks to the Lord for allowing us a safe trip. I gave that a hearty A-MEN. Fred greeted all his relatives warmly. All of them seemed genuinely happy to see each other. I was introduced to all the family members.

There was MaMa, the Colonel's wife, MaMa Panyin, the elder MaMa of the family living in the house and Ursula (daughter of the Ekubans) who when older will evolve from MaMa to MaMa

Panyin. Later I would find that the Colonel and his wife were not Fred's relatives... but family friends of the Ekubans.

My first Ghanaian meal was kenkey, fried plantain and some kind of sauce. Kenkey is made from ground corn, and it is a staple dish for the Akan, Ga, and Ewe tribes of West Africa. Kenkey is similar to a sourdough dumpling. Oh! I had my first glass of Ghanaian water. There was no discernible difference from what I drink in America. I asked the Colonel about the London drinking water. The first words from his mouth were "It is terrible".

Now how do I get the word out to the non suspecting public. The word is... *DON'T DRINK THE WATER... IN LONDON TOWN.* We talked a bit more and finally said good night. I eagerly looked forward to sleeping. I had been cat napping for the past 24 hours.

Before going to bed, water was put in a bucket for showering or washing. Fred thought that I would bolt at this. No problem. For me, this experience goes back to growing up in Indiana without many of the accepted conveniences. I have not forgotten having to heat water and then pouring it into the tin tub which was used to wash clothes and also to bathe. I must add the Ekubans are much better off than that. They are not suffering. Water for showering/bathing was not working.

Monday, August 3 - Sleep was great. I am uncertain as to the exact time that we awakened. It was close to 10 a.m. That was 6 a.m. in New Jersey. Breakfast was prepared. We had eggs with bread, lettuce and tomatoes.

That morning, Sister Nana, the sister of Mrs. Ekuban, had come by the house. She and Adolph accompanied Fred and me in the car. After breakfast, we went to Mr. Ekuban's (Nana Sam's) paper supply company. Fred drove Mr. Ekuban's Volkswagen. Traffic was heavy.

To me, the drivers were quite reckless... not unlike New York City. Whenever traffic slowed down, a vendor would appear at your window, usually the passenger side, selling almost every item imaginable... bread, tools, audio cassettes, towels, etc. Most people referred to the vendors as *hawkers*.

SEEING, LISTENING AND LEARNING

On the other side of the road, Africans were making palm wine, wood carvings, caskets, etc. They were working hard making items that people would want to buy. For each hawker, the key action was persistence, but they were never rude.

The language of Fred's father was *Ga*. His mother spoke the *Akyem language. They were both killed in a road accident.* Sister Nana and Adolph both spoke the *Fanti language.* The *Fanti, Twi and Akyem languages* are linked culturally as well as linguistically. They all fall under the *generic term... Akan.*

English is Ghana's official language. The conversation shifted from the *Ga language* to *Fanti* to *Twi* to English. After some time, I was able to understand parts of the conversation. As soon as I had picked up on a word, I would hear another word where the meanings appeared to be the same.

For example, when I thought that I was able to recognize... thank you, i.e. *medasi (Fanti)*, I would hear Fred say *O U Wa DONG (Ga)*. Fred is fluent in several languages. He suspected a person's language by the tribal marks worn by that person. Often, he would engage that person in conversation. Some few times, he guessed wrong about the person's language... but not often.

All of this was fascinating to me. On the plane, Andrew (the white medical student) had spoken about his eagerness to get to North Ghana and Kenya to see the animals. While acknowledging that seeing the animals would be nice, I told him that at this time, I am primarily interested in learning about the people... their traditions and culture. Already my goals are being met.

When we arrived at Nana Sam's office, I met Patricia Mr. Ekuban's secretary. Patricia, was nice and quite attractive. To me, one of her most appealing attributes was her deeply black skin obviously positively influenced by the hot Ghanaian sun. There was no dearth of black skinned people here. How could anyone... white or black... ever suggest that to be *black* is to be *ugly?* How could anyone... white or black... ever believe it?

Patricia greeted me with a voice that was conspicuously pleasant to my ear and led me to an adjoining office where I was seated and brought a glass of water. Fred went to another room to conduct some sort of business. Adolph opted to wait outside near the car. Sister Nana sat with me and talked... about church.

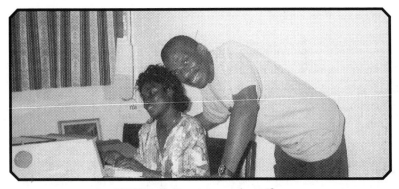

Will with Patricia at the office

When Fred returned, he told me that should I have to make a phone call back to the U.S., I could use the phone in Mr. Ekuban's office.

SEEING, LISTENING AND LEARNING

(OBEISANCE)

Now is the time to begin Fred's *Obeisance* which is rendering tribute to highly thought of family members and friends. Finally I am beginning to understand why Fred had 8 pieces of luggage. For the next few days, he will give money, clothes, material, jewelry and other gifts fulfilling his obligation... *obeisance to those recognized.*

The first day we visited Sister Nana's pastor who pastors a Pentecostal church. This was not an obeisance visit. In the states, Fred had been trying to purchase some religious books for the pastor and gave him a progress report. It seems that there were several volumes, and the minister would have to decide which one(s) he wanted.

In his memo pad, Fred wrote down the information. When that was done, the minister suggested that we read scripture from the Bible. Fortunately... or... unfortunately, I did not bring my reading glasses and therefore was unable to participate. Fred could... and did.

He read from Matthew in the new testament. Now remember... this is no excuse, but I had been awake almost 24 hours before last night's sleep. Shortly, my eyelids became very heavy. I fought fiercely to keep them open.

Fred would read, and the minister would interpret, and then the loop would repeat itself. I stretched my eyes and warded off a yawn. Reading scripture and interpreting continued. Fred asked, "Are God and Jesus one and the same". Minister Jonathan Nyquey replied, "yes".

"Well" said Fred, "When Jesus died on the cross, God must have also died". I thought I sensed some uncertainty on the minister's part as he uttered something... I am not sure what.

By now, I was more awake. Other people were waiting for sessions with the reverend. Our visit was therefore cut short. We concluded our gathering with a prayer. The reverend was praying in one of the languages. After which, we sang. That's right... WE sang 'Lift up Your Hand'.

The reverend let Fred know that he would appreciate a few items of clothing... a blazer and a 3 piece suit allowing him to change up now and then. Fred had agreed to buy the books... but not clothing. A-Men to that!

We drove to many different areas where Fred had to deliver gifts. Sometimes the roads were dirt, sometimes paved and often our route took us very near the Gulf of Guinea, and we could see the fishermen launching their boats and returning at the end of the day.

From where we were, you could walk into the gulf. The boats were canoes, but they had motors which would be removed when the fishermen returned home. Many women could be seen skillfully carrying groceries, clothes, water, etc. in different sized containers on their heads. Although not often, there were times when you would see men transporting merchandise on their heads.

Some areas seemed economically 'well to do'. However there were poor areas and others even more poor. There was a certain smell permeating the air. The odor was similar to what I had smelled in several Mississippi towns. One of which was the place where I was born. Some of the Ghanaian areas reminded me very much of some of those Mississippi towns. It was quite evident that the Ghana economy was not thriving in every area.

(AKWAABA)

At every home we visited, someone would seat us and bring a glass of water. Following the water, would be a cold soft drink. Sister Nana explained that the custom should be observed by taking at least a sip of the water. The soft drink could be refused. The tradition was referred to as the *Akwaaba* (Welcome).

Sometimes when our visit was with one of the elders, Fred would be expected to kneel at the feet of the elder while they talked a bit. Knowing that I would tease him about this, Fred would try to stifle a slight chuckle. Almost every time I shook hands with a person, that person would conclude the shake by holding the tips of his/her fingers to my fingertips and snapping them together.

I asked Fred the significance of the hand shake. He did not know, but suggested that it was something done by the young. If so, it certainly had caught on because age seemed not be an indicator as to whether or not the *finger snapping* would take place. Almost everyone I met seemed to do it.

SEEING, LISTENING AND LEARNING

(COLONEL NAPOLEON)

Later that night, I sat down and talked with the Colonel who preferred to be called *Colonel Napoleon*. By his admission, his years as a youth could only be classified as wild, but now he is active in the Pentecostal church. With respect to conflict, his philosophy is now... dialogue.

The colonel had spent 21 years in Ghana's army and air force. He was able to retire from the military. When the UN. was in the Congo, he was there with the Ghanaian force. Unequivocally, the colonel states that the CIA was involved in the 1961 assassinations of Patrice Lumumba, the Congo leader, and Dag Hammarskjold, the Secretary General of the UN.

After breaking into UN quarters (where liquor was stored), in the Congo, and becoming intoxicated, the colonel says that he was slated to face a firing squad for his crime. On the day that he was to be executed, the man scheduled to man the machine gun became intoxicated. When the machine gunner was ready to fire, a white American officer approached the machine gunner, and the colonel was inexplicably freed.

Colonel Napoleon

Feverishly he looked for the American to thank him. He could never find him. During another crisis (undefined), he again saw the American officer who revealed himself as Jesus. The officer (Jesus?) had silver and white hair. By this time, I found it difficult waiting for him to conclude the story. I asked... *did he resemble that white man that I see in so many illustrations?* The colonel could only say that no one can say whether Jesus is black, white, Aryan or anything else.

There was another 'story' that the colonel told to me. Before going to war in the Congo, he and four of his army comrades had gone to see the Juju Man. The Juju man is revered and thought to have magical powers... what many in the West refer to as 'black magic'. To ensure a safe return from the war, the Juju Man had insisted that it would be necessary to cut up their body parts. Colonel Napoleon refused.

The Juju Man cut up the body parts of his four comrades and put them in a vat. Later the colonel would see the four leave the Juju's place... completely whole... identical to the form they had when they walked into the place. They went to battle, and all survived... including the colonel. After the war the four died in non threatening although bizarre incidents, e.g. one stepped off a curb only to be hit by a non speeding car... another fell dead while shopping at the Bukom Market.

After hearing of the deaths of two of his allies, another soldier immediately dropped dead. Finally the fourth soldier died when he decided to re-enlist in the army. After signing the papers, he too fell dead. The colonel concluded that there is always a price to pay by those who consort with Satan's agents.

Colonel Napoleon told me of his involvement in the Kwame Nkrumah coup d'etat. Although unwilling to participate, he knew that for him, it was *do or die*. When the coup began, another officer came to his room and ordered "let's go". Responding, the colonel made it known that he had no gun. The officer told him he expected that response and had therefore brought a gun for him.

After the successful coup, Colonel Napoleon was called before his commanding officers to be executed, because he was thought to be loyal to Kwame Nkrumah. The officer who had brought the gun to the colonel vouched for him by saying, *"He is not loyal to Nkrumah and was an active participant in the coup. I saw him"*. When Ghana gained its independence from the British in 1957, Kwame Nkrumah was Ghana's first head of state.

Ghana has had several coups. The Senior Officers pulled one. Then the Junior Officers ousted the Senior Officers. Flight Lieutenant J. J. Rawlings, the current head of state, took over, stepped down and again seized control of the government. Newspaper reports hint that after 11 years, Mr. Rawlings is slated to again step down. At this time, Ghana is under military rule.

Colonel confides that he was once offered a position in the government as the Secretary of State and at another time offered an ambassadorship. Amarkai was shocked and surprised that the colonel spoke so freely with me. Amarkai claims to know only that the colonel had a reputation for being a fierce guerrilla fighter in the Ghanaian army.

Oh! Colonel Napoleon said that soldiers feared being placed in front of him. The soldiers felt that they would surely be killed. When an enemy was behind him, he could sense that he was going to be fired on. He has been wounded.

His left eye seems to be impaired. Fellow soldiers referred to him as the *soldier who could not be killed.*

TORTO

(A PUBLIC SERVANT)

Tuesday, August 4 - Today there are more obeisance visits. We are still awaiting the return of Mr. & Mrs. Ekuban. They are still in the USA. I think they are scheduled to return Sunday, August 9. Mr. Ekuban knows the whereabouts of the transformer needed to convert from 110 to 220 volts necessary to charge the batteries of our camcorders. In addition to the difference in voltage, the shape of the plug also differs. We have not been able to use our camcorders.

Tomorrow we will see another of the elders. Within 48 hours of arrival, visitors must register at the Ghana Office of Immigration. We were not immediately aware of the deadline since we were slow in reading the registration forms we had gotten upon arrival.

Amarkai has a friend, Torto, who is a Ghana public servant. Torto lived in the USA about ten years ago. Amarkai wanted to meet with him to learn how he could get his two hundred dollar deposit returned. All along, Amarkai knew that he would not return with his camcorder since he had agreed to give it to Mr. Ekuban.

Torto believes in and is a practitioner of... Voodoo. I don't know that Amarkai expects Voodoo to get back his deposit... hmm... perhaps. A suggestion that Torto made to Amarkai was that he should have used his Ghanaian passport (eliminating his status as a visitor). Erroneously, Amarkai thought that his Ghana passport had expired. I playfully reminded Amarkai what had been told to him at the Ghana Embassy in New York, i.e. "Ghana does not recognize dual citizenship. When one becomes an American, he/she is no longer a citizen of Ghana and is required to give up the Ghana passport". We all laughed when I told Amarkai... *Ghana no longer wants you!* The Brit has become an American.

Torto left with us to point out directions as to how we were to get to the Immigration Office. To his subordinates, he announced "I am leaving for awhile and will return shortly". In unison, they all responded "yes sir". We left.

Torto wore a uniform that had a military ring to it. His shirt was sky blue with epaulets on each shoulder. Torto's pants were grey or blue. Consistent with the military theme, his uniform was topped off with a smart looking beret. The Immigration Office was only a short distance away, so we all walked there.

Concerning the deposit, Torto thought the easiest thing to do would be to hold onto the camcorder until his deposit was returned, and then give the camcorder to Mr. Ekuban. For that advice, however good, I doubt that Torto used Voodoo.

The office was not yet open, so we sat outside and talked. Torto and Amarkai talked about old times in Ghana and in the states. While they were talking, up strode this African brother with these long blue jean pants, a leather and jean shirt and cowboy boots. His jeans appeared to be starched like my white shirts were when I was a youngster. Looking at him, seemed to increase the hot temperature by 10 degrees minimally.

With the temperature at whatever degree, I felt certain that any moment, he would break out in flames. That brother was a sight. I am not certain that he was Ghanaian. He too may have been visiting. I thought that no one else had noticed him and was attempting to internalize my pseudo concern, but it wasn't long before Amarkai and Torto leaned toward me whispering "do you see that brother".

We all broke out in a big big laugh. Laughing, I queried Torto as to the closeness of that brother's attire and Amarkai's attire when he first left Accra headed to the states. Amarkai denied it, but we had another big laugh.

What I did not share with Torto and Fred was that somehow the young man reminded me of me. Quite a few years ago, during late winter or early spring, I went to see my mother in Pulaski, Mississippi. At that time, I was living in Gary, Indiana. I packed heavy clothing reinforced by long underwear which had helped me deal with the well known heavy wind, known as the 'Hawk', in the Chicago/Gary area.

Unaware that Mississippi might be different than Gary, I suffered during my stay. The temperature was hot and I sweat although I attempted to roll up my long johns, unsuccessfully, to the knees. Although I laughed, at the brother in the jeans and leather, I also empathized.

Another brother showed up with what appeared to be his mother and sister. He wore the baggy clothes, unlaced sneakers and walked while listening to his Walkman radio. When he stood up and walked with that *gangster lean*, I needed no more proof... this guy had to be from the states.

Torto said guys in Ghana dress that way. His passport was red. Later we found that his passport was French. Soon the Immigration Office opened. Amarkai had to fill out my application since I had again forgotten my glasses.

COCONUTS, FUFU AND YAM

We have one more official stop... the American Embassy. After registering there, we will be covered in the event anything happens to our passports. Should they get lost, new ones will be issued.

The woman, who we talked with, at the embassy, was Ghanaian and very cooperative. Amarkai said that there was another woman, named Rose, who previously did that job at the embassy. According to Amarkai, Rose was not cooperative and the exact opposite of the woman currently doing the job.

We left home early this morning, missed breakfast, and hadn't yet eaten anything the whole day. While in the American Embassy, no mention was made of, nor was there the slightest inclination to stop at one of the places, in the area, serving American food. Amarkai swears that I brought potato chips from the states... In no way was that true.

On the way back to the car, we bought coconuts from a street hawker. The vendor whacked off the husk and whacked a hole in the coconut which made it easy to drink the milk. When the milk was finished, we cut out the coconut and ate that. Amarkai bought another one to take home.

That evening, we were to be treated to the meal that Ghanaians had been raving about since my arrival... fufu. Fufu is made of plantain and cassava, pounded in a mortar, and then immersed in soup. Actually, the fufu is put in a bowl, and the soup is poured over it. It is one of Ghana's staple foods.

When eating, the protocol dictates that you break off a small piece of the fufu in your hand, sop it in the soup and then swallow it. To me, it was somewhat bland, but I ate it.

A finger bowl is provided. On completing the meal, you wash your hands in the finger bowl and dry them. I thought of my Aunt Emma who would mix corn bread and pot liquor from greens with her hands and eat them. Can there be a connection?

Oh! Yesterday we ate yams. For me, it was noticeably different. The yams were less like the sweet yams that I am accustomed to eating in the U.S.... but seemed to taste more like a sweeter version of the white potato.

ABU TUM DAM POH PII

W*ednesday, August 5* - More obeisance. Our first visit was with one of the tribe elders. On different occasions, the elder has visited the states but makes it clear that after short stays, he is eager to return to Ghana. He asks my name. I thought that I knew why he had asked.

I regretted having to say... *Singleton* in an uncertain manner. He looked puzzled, and Amarkai related to him what I had said about the origin of slave names. *African names had been beaten away from the slaves. As surnames, all the slaves from a given plantation assumed the surname of the plantation owner.* Had I been able to give the elder an African name, he felt that he could tell me something about my tribal beginnings... I wanted that.

On departing, we shook hands and jointly snapped our fingertips. The elder made me promise to meet him when he again comes to America. Having to define how I got my name made me think that in all likelihood, many indigenous Africans probably know as little about us as we do about them.

We're on the road again. One thing that I forgot to mention is that when a Ghanaian attempts to get your attention, he/she sometimes utters a quiet little... *sooh... sooh* sound made with the teeth and tongue. Many vendors use that sound to get your attention.

We arrived at Amarkai's grandfather's house. He lives in a modest hovel like dwelling... but has MONEY. His name is Kweku Bronya Amparbin. When we walked in, Amarkai grabbed his hand, and the old man seemed to light up as he vigorously swung Amarkai's hand. Together they sang a tribal song... *abu tum dam poh pii...abu tum dam poh pii.*

They were really into it. It was as though they were not cognizant of my presence, and only the two of them were in the room. When their initial celebration had ended, Amarkai introduced me to him. Immediately, and with equal enthusiasm, the old man grabbed my hand, swung it vigorously and sang the tribal song... *abu tum dam poh pii... abu tum dam poh pii.*

As he smiled, you could see the empty spaces in his mouth where teeth had once been. He had a strong... strong grip. The interaction seemed so genuine. After awhile, the old one went to the rear of his house and returned with a big glass of water.

He wanted to *pay tribute,* i.e. pour libation to the gods and our ancestors thanking them for allowing us a safe flight from the U.S. to Ghana and requesting a safe return flight. Additionally, he thanked them for allowing ME the opportunity to come back home. Although a Christian, the old man still adheres to some traditions not linked with Christianity, e.g. pouring libation. His Christian name is Emanuel.

Kweku Bronya Amparbin, the elder, would chant something while dancing around... and pour libation on the floor. Chanting, dancing, and pouring continued until the glass was empty. I am told that on more formal occasions, alcohol is used for pouring libation.

Will and Kwesi Bronya Amparbin (abu tum dam poh pii)

Amarkai, sneaking a glance at me to see how I was taking it, bowed at the feet of the elder and presented him with several gifts, e.g., shirts, pants, material, alcoholic beverages, etc. A teenager, the old one's great grandson, walked into the house. It seems that he and Amarkai had not seen each other since the teen was a very young boy.

When we were ready to leave, Amarkai gave his young relative some money. An interesting, I think, thing happened. The young man gave the money to the old one. Tradition dictates that before the young man can spend the money, the old one must give his approval.

As I walked toward the door, the old one turned in my direction. Amarkai told me that he was blind and to extend my hand to the elder and take his. I was shocked. Until that moment, I had no idea that he was blind. As we touched hands, again we went through the dance and tribal song... *Abu tum dam poh pii... abu tum dam poh pii.*

Once again he gripped my hand with such great force, and again there was no threat of harm, but there was magnetism suggesting empathy and kinship. As we concluded, we shook hands warmly and jointly snapped our fingertips. His final words to me were... "Now you and I are one". I was indeed moved.

I asked Amarkai the meaning of the words from the tribal song, i.e. *Abu tum dam poh pii*. He thought for awhile (I guess that's what he was doing) and said "United we Stand". I laughed at that immediately and insisted that he stop lying and admit that he just doesn't know.

Amarkai's ebony skin attempted, unsuccessfully, to blush. It was true. He did not know, and we both laughed. Amarkai did say that he would find out. His grandfather was born on Christmas day. The Bronya in his name is a Ga word for Christmas. The old man was born on Christmas day which fell on Sunday hence the name

Kwesi. One of Amarkai's aunts lives near the old one's house, so we stopped there. She owned a little restaurant that seemed to be doing well. There were more than a few customers in the restaurant. This is the aunt who once carried *Little Amarkai* strapped to her back.

When the aunt mentioned that, Amarkai leaned toward me and whispered that I congratulate her since that was customary. I blew everyone's mind when I quickly said... *Ayiko* (Ah yee ko) which is Fanti and translates *"you have done well"*. *Those in the restaurant immediately and gleefully responded yaaei (yah yay).*

Amarkai was shocked. Before we left America, he had taught me to use that response when a compliment seemed appropriate. I was quite surprised that it came to me at that convenient moment. In my view, Amarkai's hue, which reflected a true son of equatorial Africa, may have actually reddened a bit... not in embarrassment but pleasant surprise... whew.

Everyone laughed, and the applause was spontaneous. The aunt shook my hand, and I felt good. Amarkai's aunt is married to one of the village chiefs. One week from Sunday, which is August 16, she invited us to come hear the chief decide a village dispute. Additionally, she asked what would I like to eat on that day. My reply was fried plantain and yam.

CULTURE SHOCK

On our way home, Amarkai stopped at a body shop to price the repair of the side of the car. It seems that Theophilus, his nephew, tried to move the car after his mother had told him not to touch it while she was away. His mom, Rex, is still in the U.S. Theo is worried that he is going to get one of those down home... good old fashioned behind whippings when she returns. Uncle Amarkai is supposed to intercede in his behalf.

I trust that Amarkai was able to get some kind of commitment at the repair shop. In any event, we headed home. All of Fred's nephews (Adolph, Theo, Joy, Fred) seem to be well behaved and bright. One, or another, will always make sure we get whatever we need. Only a few minutes ago, Joy brought us some apple juice.

Melody, one of Amarkai's nieces, asked how I enjoyed the food. Her name describes the tone of her voice. It is surely melodious. She opened up the door to the porch, so I could sit out there and write. In a few minutes, she returned with a thick pillow. The pillow was used to prop up my feet. There is much to be said for the *old order where man is king*. To Melody, I said *medasi*.

Joy came to the porch and asked if I wanted to watch the soccer match on TV. It was the 1992 Olympics, and Ghana was matched up against Spain. Before I got close to the television, I could hear cheers... and groans. Everyone in the house was really into the game.

Before falling asleep, I think I watched more of a soccer game than I ever had at any other time. Of course, I too was rooting for Ghana. Alas, Spain won the match... 2 to nil (2 to zero).

Let's talk about culture shock. I watched the commercials on TV. They dealt with OMO Washing Powder, Yogurt, ABC Super Malt, King Soap, Nestles Corelac, Vaseline, EMS Delivery Service, Drustan Analgesic Tablets, Carnation Milk, Femeur Cosmetics and Pioneer Metal.

Only EMS Delivery Service had a white involved in its commercial. He did seem to be the boss, but everyone else in that commercial was black. All the other commercials were 100% unadulterated... black African. Hey! Not bad. By the way, the younger children recited the commercials from memory.

For the news, there was an African man and an African woman. Another African man gave the weather. It seems that the broadcast media is controlled by the government. In the event of another coup, you can be sure that there will be a strong effort to gain control of the broadcast media.

The colonel won't watch the news. He said all of it is orchestrated by the government. I started to write again when Joy asked if I would like to walk to the junction. I said... yes.

Outside, the night was dark, but hey... this is not the USA. Joy told me of an atomic energy plant a few miles down the road. He talked about the cultural things in Accra... the University of Ghana, the bank, hospitals, atomic power, etc. Joy wants to study in the U.S. Sunday, the day we arrived, was his sixteenth birthday.

Before I forget, the younger ones wanted me to say something in the Fanti language before leaving the house for the walk. Joy had prepared me for this. I am ready... I think. Since I had passed where they were standing, I turned my head and yelled back to them... *mE kaw maaba*. That means... I am going, and I will be back.

They had a big laugh. Earlier they had heard me respond *medasi* when Melody brought me a foot stool. When I said it, I thought it was *Twi*. Joy says that *medasi* is Fanti. Later Fred would tell me that they were interchangeable.

Joy said that he had spoken with his family about a holiday in America. They suggested that he study hard and earn a scholarship there. When the teacher is not around, Joy thinks that more students are becoming unruly. I was somewhat surprised when he opined that armed robbers sometimes lurk in the bushes to take your money.

Furthermore, he added, when in the market place, you should hold tightly to your money because pickpockets abound. Sometimes they attempt to grab your money and run. Should you follow that person and catch up with him, he may have allies waiting to help him beat you up.

Although it was dark, and there were no street lights, I had felt safe until that moment. Tightly, I clutched my pocket where I had money and showed much more concern as people passed us on the dark road. Joy even started jumping at unexpected sounds.

Inwardly, I fought off a smile since I was warned more about this area in Ghana than 17th and 25th (fondly referred to as One Seven and Two Five) in Gary. They were said to be two of Gary's roughest districts. One seven was the area where I grew up, and I never feared walking the streets there.

Joy talked about the good things Kwame Nkrumah had done for Ghana. Joy seemed to think that the Ashanti had opposed Nkrumah because there seemed to be so many Ga and Fanti supporting him. Using Joy's words, "The Ashanti labeled the Ga and Fanti as being good with their brains".

Science is what Joy wants to study. When we returned to the house, I exclaimed... *maaba*. That means *I am back*. Again the youngsters laugh. Friday, Joy wants to take me to Accra. That sounds good to me, and I readily agree.

Thursday, August 6 - I told Fred about my conversation with Joy. Expanding a bit, Fred mentioned that the Fanti are usually associated with education. Most of Ghana's teachers are Fanti. It seems that the missionaries set up the first secondary schools for Ghanaians at Cape Coast which happened to be a Fanti stronghold.

Now that the missionary issue has arisen, I suppose that it is time for an editorial comment. In driving around Accra, I saw signs promoting Christianity. I saw a host of churches of various Christian denominations, e.g., Methodist, Baptist, Pentecostal, Catholic. Cars, busses and vans had decals and paintings alluding to Jesus.

One decal that seemed to epitomize the thoughts of many Ghanaians who were Christian... and there seemed to be many read "Trust in Jesus your miracle is coming".

In America, we Africans... yes Africans know that our names, particularly surnames, have absolutely nothing at all to do with us or choice. I asked some of the Ghanaians... *where there names, e.g., Fred, Patricia, came from.*

Interesting enough the reply was "When I was baptized, I took on a Christian name". For me, I would call that MISSIONARY POWER. Now here we have people, minimally with more longevity than Europeans, allowing outsiders to come in and tell them that their indigenous religions are no good. Furthermore Africans should convert to *their Christianity.*

This is not to say that the one God concept is European. Now I am by no means anti Christ, but there seems to be a certain arrogance associated with those missionaries particularly those who seemed to dwindle when comparing their being Christ like with those they converted.

When the *new* Catholic is confirmed, he/she may take on another *Christian* name. For example, Fred becomes... *Fred Winston.* At least Ghanaians know and keep the father's surname. Nii Amarkai Laryea upon becoming a Christian and being confirmed becomes *Fred Winston Laryea.*

It seems that when the *new* Christian is in school, he/she is encouraged to use the *Christian name.* At home, they are sometimes still called by the tribal name. Fred said that if we were together, in the states, and met Africans who he knows from Ghana, they would call him *Fred* in deference to what he is probably called at work.

From this time on, I told Fred... oops, I mean Amarkai, that even at work, I WILL NOT refer to him as Fred. Under all circumstances, to me, his name will be Amarkai. In many instances, African Americans are seeking names from the continent, and many from the continent are seeking English names.

GYE NYAME

This morning, after breakfast, we drove Theophilus and Joy to school. They are attending the Atchimota School, which is purported to be one of Accra's better schools, this summer. After dropping them off, we pass some prisoners doing hard labor on the side of the road. According to Amarkai, they don't earn one coin while doing time which is often 'hard time'.

Amarkai had to exchange some money, so we stopped at the Bank for Housing and Construction. When you have larger U.S. bills, e.g., 50's or 100's, you get a better rate when exchanging them for the Ghanaian cedi.

Somehow, the rationale is related to Ghanaian traders going to Lagos, Nigeria to make purchases. When the Nigerians receive smaller bills, they want to cash them in for larger bills, so they won't have to carry wads of small bills to Europe and America. That was the explanation a banker gave to me. There may be more to the explanation since I wonder whether *big money people* would want to carry monetary bills... big or small when there is *plastic*.

Perhaps my thinking has been tinged by the western world. I must watch that. Anyway, today's rate is 448 cedis for one U.S. dollar... that is for big bills. With smaller bills, the rate is 440 cedis for one U.S. dollar.

After leaving the bank, we went to see *Psycho Marx* an old friend of Amarkai. Other than saying that *Psycho* is a crazy guy, no other explanation was given for the name. *Psycho* welcomed me to Ghana adding that *Isaac Hayes* had been to Ghana to see the *slave castles*.

Viewing the *slave castles* conjured up images that caused *Isaac Hayes* to weep profusely.

Stevie Wonder had also visited Ghana. Amarkai told Psycho that he wanted to get the car repaired before Mrs. Ekuban returned home. On hearing that, the first words from Psycho's mouth were "She is going to beat A-S-S". *Psycho* did not spell out the word.

To find out about the repair, we went to Volty's Volkswagen place. Fortunately, Amarkai knew the manager who told him that they send the cars out for body repair. The manager told Amarkai that he would take him to the place where the work is done. In that way, the middle man could be eliminated.

After minor negotiations, it was agreed that the car would be repaired by Saturday. Now that the car is gone, we have to travel by taxi. Amarkai, Adolph and I walked over to the Ekuban's paper supply company. We drank water and a soft drink. Ghanaians refer to a soft drink as *mineral*.

From there, we walked to a nearby FOREX. FOREX is an acronym for foreign exchange. Amarkai needed more money.

Front view of 1000 cedis - at that time ~$2.22

Back view of 1000 cedis

We talked to the exchange person who was interested in expanding his business. He asked us about buying, in the U.S., reasonably priced cosmetics at wholesale prices. Neither of us were able to give him any pertinent information.

We caught a taxi and rode to the Kotoka Airport area. On the side of the road, an African was carving wooden objects. Approaching the site, Amarkai and I saw and liked the carving... a chief's stool that had just been completed. On either side of the stool was a carved symbol. I was told that the symbol meant GyE Nyame. The English translation is *Except God... Symbol of the omnipotence and immortality of God.*

Initially, we were told that the stool would cost 35,000 cedis. Shortly, he quoted a price of 30,000 cedis. Amarkai asked about my certainty in wanting the stool. I was certain. Amarkai made a counter offer of 25,000 cedis assuring the vendor that I would buy at that price. The carver's face suggested that he was not pleased with that offer. After a brief discussion, they agreed on the 25,000 cedis price. Amarkai also wanted one of the stools, so he put in an order at the same price. He left a deposit of 4,000 cedis. The carver's parting request was "If anyone asks, please say that you paid 30,000 cedis for the stool.

With our rate of exchange, 25,000 cedis, the amount I paid, equates to approximately $55.81. I want the chief's stool to be something that will pass from generation to generation in my family... not necessarily due to death. The *how and when* will have to be something that I decide on later.

GyE Nyame chief's stool

To get back to North Legon, we caught another taxi. On arrival, Adolph went to the trunk of the taxi, unloaded the stool and took it into the house. To Adolph, I was most sincere in saying *medasi*.

THAWING OUT

For dinner, we had jollof rice and fried plantain. After dinner, we sat down to watch the *tellie*. The youngsters had been watching a vampire movie and for some reason, they left the room. Colonel decided that he had enough of vampires and removed the cassette from the VCR.

The Colonel inserted one of his own cassettes, and to my surprise, on the screen appeared one of those TV evangelists. I don't recall his name, but the name did sound Jewish.

Before long, I felt that I would fall asleep. Watching the evangelist seemed to do the trick. I remember Joy shaking me and suggesting that I go to my room and sleep. That seemed to perk me up, and I noticed that the room again seemed full. Joy, Adolph, Theophilus, Fred, Akos (the maid), Ursula and Mamefia were all in the room. Their big guns were firing. Question after question was asked of me. Ursula continued to ask questions for me to answer, but all the questions were directed to Joy.

Continually, she urged me to speak Fanti. She was on the offense. I suggested that she dialogue with me in English, and we could discuss Fanti meanings and translations. This seemed to surprise her a bit, but slowly she complied.

Ursula is thirteen years old. Her birthday is April 23. "Is this your first trip to Africa?" Yes, I replied. "Why?" She would ask. "What are you writing in that book?" For each answer, she would again ask... "why". "Why didn't your son come?" "Did he want to come?"

Her school has not yet recessed. Ursula wanted to know if I would drive her to school tomorrow. I told her that Uncle Amarkai had put the car in the shop. She suggested that I borrow the Colonel's truck. Finally she asked "Can you drive?" My reply was... I think so, but I don't know what the Colonel's plans are for tomorrow.

I was wearing sneakers. Ursula and Joy wanted to know why I didn't wear sandals when in the house as Africans are wont to do. I told them that I hadn't given it much thought although I generally put on sandals when I am in the bedroom. Then I stated that Uncle Amarkai does not put on sandals. There was a noticeable lull... before replying in unison... "You don't have to put on sandals and neither does Uncle Amarkai".

To me, that episode was humorous. Incidentally, they didn't say "Uncle Amarkai". What they actually said was "Uncle Fred".

Mamefia seems a bit more shy. She doesn't say very much, but she shyly told me that she was in the sixth grade. Oh! Ursula wanted to know why I got out of bed so late. I asked her *at what time, she thought that I got up.* "6 a.m." Ursula said. *At what time, do you get up?...* I asked her. "2 a.m." she said. Joy quickly interjected... "Yes, but after school preparation, you go back to bed until 6 a.m.".

I told Ursula that when it is 6 a.m. in Ghana, it is 2 a.m. in New Jersey. We then talked about comparable times in other U.S. time zones. Joy informed me that Colonel was holding the nightly prayer meeting. Tonight will be my first. Most often, I had been out... *Oh well, let's get it on.*

Colonel recited the twenty third Psalms and then prayed. Young Fred, Mr. Ekuban's youngest son, prayed. Ursula prayed. We sang two songs. I don't remember the names, but the second was more familiar. The Colonel rendered, what to me seemed, the benediction. As the service was in progress, my eyes wandered around the room... as I made quasi judgments on all.

Joy was a strong participant... Adolph seemed mildly interested... Ursula was involved... Young Fred was going along with the program... Mamefia was participating with indecipherable fervor... Melody exuded an aura of polite concentration... Maama seemed to exhibit that old down home religion... Theophilus was totally disinterested... The Colonel was most definitely in charge... As for me, Will, you make the judgment on that.

Joy wanted to know if I would walk with him down to the junction to buy bread. I said sure. When I went outside, all the boys were there. You could argue that they were seeking relief after the prayer meeting. I have no idea, but Theo did say "this place is boring".

As we walked, they asked about the states, racism, etc. "What did I think of Ghana?" They all wanted to visit the U.S. Of particular interest were their desires to visit historical sites, such as... Lincoln's Tomb, Washington's Monument, Independence Hall, etc. My first question was... *Did they know who Christopher Columbus was?* They gave pat answers about his discovering America.

To offer an alternate view was a compulsion to which I succumbed. Additionally, I stated what I believed to be one of the rallying points of racism, i.e. the stated belief that *Africa and hence Africans have made no significant contribution to the betterment of Man.* My next question asked them to recall any.

When no answer was forthcoming, I led the conversation to what I had read in Van Sertima's 'They Came Before Columbus'... where he discussed an African presence in the Americas, before Columbus, and their contributions to existing civilizations in the Americas.

They seemed to be impressed, and when we returned home, I allowed them to leaf through the book. In the group, Theo seemed the most interested. Before going to bed, I watched tellie (television). I noticed that the movies were not interrupted by commercials. That

I assumed was because the television media was controlled by the government. *Adentsia*. That means... *I'll see you tomorrow.*

Friday, August 7 - Amarkai and the colonel left early this morning. I was still in bed. Soon, I heard a light knock on the door. I said *come in.* In walked Joy, he wanted to know if we were still going into Accra. Of course, I said, but Amarkai wanted to go with us when we went to look for kente cloth. Kente cloth is hand woven in Ghana. The cloth has an assortment of colors with varied designs. Traditionally kente cloth is worn, by men and women, on important ceremonial and religious occasions.

Joy wanted to know if we should wait until another day. No, I said. We can still go someplace. Since I had been in bed, Joy told me that he had waited until I got out of bed before he started to prepare himself for the outing. He then left the room.

I laid down on the floor to do my back exercises. Shortly, there was another light knock on the door. When I beckoned the knocker to come in, I saw that Joy had returned. "Please" he said, "Is there anything you wish me to iron for you". *No thanks* was my reply.

Joy also wanted to know what he should wear. For the occasion, I suggested trousers and a light shirt. *Hey Wes! Do you believe it? Since our arrival, today will be the first time that I will have worn long pants.*

Who's wearing short pants?

This morning I woke up singing:

This is my story
This is my song
Praising the savior
All the day long.

Uh oh! It seems to be getting to me.

Joy and I walked up to the junction. I heard Joy utter a very quiet "sooh... sooh", and a taxi stopped. The driver charged us 800 cedis to take us to Tesano where Joy was going to get a haircut.

I was elated to get out of the taxi. The kindest remark that I can make concerning the driver is that he drove wildly. As for the barber shop, it was made from old sacks... I think they were sown together. Somehow the sacks were attached to trees/sticks stuck into the ground. That was the roof.

One could enter the shop through the spaces between the trees/sticks. Inside the shop, there were a couple of handmade stools... not state of the art... and certainly not carved. There were also a couple of handmade tables where the barbers kept their tools. The tools were combs, scissors and razor blades. To cut hair, the barber held the razor blade next to, and even with, the lower teeth of the comb. The comb and razor blade together were carefully stroked down the head. Styling was very similar to what you see in the USA... you know the bowl with hair on the top and varying degrees of hair elsewhere.

Joy and I shared a stool while we waited for his turn. In bopped Adolph, Theo and another of their friends. You know the look... baggy pants and shirts with their sneakers unlaced. When they sat down, there was constant chatter. They were not boisterous, but they talked, laughed and poked fun at each other.

Adolph sat in the friend's lap. The friend placed his arms around Adolph. No problem, other than me, no one paid much attention. I was not obvious, because I had observed/heard about this phenomenon. It is not uncommon to see African men behave in this manner toward each other. Such behavior, holding hands, etc is in no way associated with homosexuality.

They continued to horse around. By now, Theo was in the chair, and the other two poked fun at him. Joy was finally finished with his cut. Since we had earlier gone to the FOREX for a money exchange, we could now be on our way. Today's rate at the FOREX was 445 cedis for one dollar.

As we exited the shop, Colonel, Amarkai, Sister Nana and Melody drove by in the truck. We waved the Colonel down, and he stopped to chat with us. During our conversation, I told him that we were headed for Accra. I spoke to the ladies... Amarkai and I pounded fists.

Joy and I headed in one direction... the truck took off in the opposite direction. We passed the barber shop. Adolph, Theo and friend were still in the shop.

Joy waved down a taxi and asked him if he were going to Accra. The driver said no, but he would take us for 600 cedis. Without hesitation, I offered to pay 500 cedis... He drove away. On our way to Tesano, Joy made no attempt to negotiate with the taxi driver. Since this was my first opportunity to negotiate, I felt compelled to do so.

Most of the taxis were going to Nkrumah Circle but not to Accra. My confidence was waning, and I began to think that we should have accepted the 600 cedi offer. At last, a taxi willing to take us to Accra stopped. His offer of a fare to us was 240 cedis... for both of us. The offer was so much lower than our first offer that there was no effort to negotiate. Readily, I agreed. Let's go. One fellow, a schoolmate of Joy's, was already in the taxi. Additionally, there was a woman, with boxes that she placed in the trunk, who was sharing the taxi with us. The woman was dressed in traditional African garb with a matching headset.

Her outfit was multicolored, and there was a sash like item wrapped around her waist. She sat next to me and appeared tired. Her closeness made it quite apparent... that she had probably been working very hard this day. On the dashboard of the taxi a 'Repent' sign was displayed. I don't know that the driver's mode was due to the condition of the taxi, i.e. last legs, but the driver drove quite sanely. PRAISE THE LORD!

Accra was busy. Vendors, hawkers, etc. were everywhere. Until today, I had not seen many Muslims identifiable by dress, but today there were many Muslims in Accra. I was told that quite a large number of Muslims live in that part of Accra. Hawkers would pass and sometimes hold up their merchandise for us to see.

Believe me! There were wall to wall vendors. Joy, who speaks like a proper British gentleman, informed me that a few of the bottom buttons on my shirt were not buttoned. *So?... I asked sarcastically.* Said Joy... "They should not be open". *Thanks so much... I said.*

That little incident caused me to remember what had happened earlier at the barber shop. When it was his turn to get his hair cut, he got up from the stool that we both occupied. Turning toward me, his instructions were... "You may turn and sit properly now". I laughed while thanking him for his permission.

We continued down the Accra streets. In front of us was a Kingsway Department Store, and Joy suggested that we go in. Outside the store, a woman was selling post cards. I bought some and put my hand in my pocket to get money to pay her. When I paid her, she smiled and very kindly warned me to beware of pickpockets. I thanked her.

As we walked the stairs to the second floor of the department store, we passed a sign which read 'LOOK OUT FOR PICKPOCKETS!' Within a few minutes, I had two warnings concerning pickpockets. Obviously that is a common problem.

While walking, I saw a man whose body appeared to be covered with a white substance. Amarkai and I had seen men and women 'clad' similarly. They wore traditional clothing, but their bodies seemed covered with a white substance. Amarkai told me that the substance is a white clay substance that is called ayilo (ah' yee loe).

The men and women so clad are referred to as fetish priests and fetish priestesses. The white clay indicates that they are protected by the ancestral spirits. Any challenge to them is taken at the challenger's own risk. One may see them sprinkling the clay on the ground. That is an invitation for the other spirits to join them. Additionally they are indicating that ayilo is good for them and Mother Earth (considered a deity). I thought it interesting that there seemed to be no gender conflict in that religion. Males and females seemed to assume the priesthood.

The fetish priest(ess) is thought to be the source between spirits and the living. Women who are pregnant sometimes crave for ayilo to eat. It is said to provide calcium and iron.

We approached a section where soft drinks (minerals) and snacks were sold. I asked Joy what he wanted. He said "Mirinda". For us, I ordered two Mirindas and some cookies (biscuits) for Joy. Perhaps I was thirsty, and I ordered another Mirinda. Mirinda seems to be some kind of orange soda. I am uncertain as to Mirinda being the flavor or the name of the company making the mineral. As we walked through the store, I was inattentive with respect to prices of items, so I am unable to make valid comparisons. Hopefully, we will get a chance to return to Kingsway.

Outside again, we walked to the Bank of Housing and Construction. Although it was under construction, we passed the library where Joy does much of his studying. While walking down the street, a woman approached us. She was swinging a stick wildly as she ranted and raved about something. Pedestrians gave her room. After passing us, she picked up something and crashed it to the ground. Someone, Joy, uttered "That is a mad (insane) woman". I agreed. Several times, we passed men walking together and holding hands... women too. Shortly we passed the Holy Spirit Cathedral and the Psychiatric Hospital. I asked Joy whether or not the mad woman should be in the Psychiatric Hospital. "When she gets a little worse" was Joy's response.

Another place we visited was the UCT Department Store. Very near us, a taxi stopped to let out a passenger. For 800 cedis, the driver agreed to take us home to North Legon. We are on our way, and the driver drives quite sanely.

The smallest bill in my pocket was 1,000 cedis. At North Legon, the driver claimed not to have change when I attempted to pay him. Frantically, I searched my pockets and could only come up with 600 cedis. Joy had 200 cedis, and together we paid him.

In the house, I looked, unsuccessfully, in the bedroom, for 200 cedis to repay Joy. From my pocket, I took out 500 cedis and gave it to Joy. It wasn't much, but he had profited and was uncomplaining.

For dinner, we had some kind of corn. Someone told me that the corn was roasted and sent to the corn mill to be ground into a brownish powder. Three to four teacups of the powder are put into a pot containing palm soup, i.e. juice from palm fruit, and stirred continuously for twenty to twenty five minutes. It is stirred until it becomes a yellowish or brownish paste. At that time, it is rolled into serving sizes and served. In the Fanti language, the meal is called *Aprepensa*.

That evening, I met another *Uncle Fred*. Fred Ekuban, who lives in Central Ghana, was visiting, and he is a part of the *extended family*. Fred is a medical technician. We talked about marriage... he is engaged. Additionally, our conversation touched on DuBois, Malcolm X and AIDS. My impression was that Fred was a very nice and friendly young man.

He went into the living room to see the remainder of the Ghana vs. Australia soccer game. Ghana was victorious... 1 to nil. By defeating Australia, Ghana became the bronze medal winner at the 1992 Barcelona Olympics. The household roared expressing approval of the victory.

Nii Amarkai Laryea came in. He and the Colonel had been hanging out today. With Amarkai accompanying him, Colonel was bent on continuing his ministry. Colonel is on the long winded side… so Amarkai hinted at catching a taxi to get home before Colonel finally decided that it was time to go.

After eating, Amarkai, Joy, Theo, young Fred, *Fulash we call him*, and I walked Fred Ekuban to the junction to catch a taxi. Before saying our good-byes, we talked awhile. As we walked back to the house, Theo revealed that he had been caught *cutting classes*. Again, he was calling on Amarkai to intervene and break the news to Mr. & Mrs. Ekuban upon their return.

Back in the house, we sat down to watch the tellie. Ursula noticed that I was wearing shoes. "Where are your sandals?"… she wanted to know. I pointed to Amarkai. Today she reprimanded him also. Sheepishly, Amarkai said "I guess we will have to wear sandals in the house". All of us shared a big hearty laugh.

Before I went to bed, Amarkai asked if I had any rubbing alcohol. I said no, but suggested that he use my after shave lotion. In a stentorian voice, he demanded that I bring it to him. *Right… I responded sarcastically. Adentsia.*

Saturday, August 8 - Nii Amarkai awakened me informing me that I had been invited to morning devotion service in the house. Here we go again. I got up, brushed my teeth, and quickly threw on some clothes. By the time I reached the living room, service had already started. Singing voices abounded.

As I passed Amarkai to reach an empty chair, his deep voice bellowed… with halfway dulcet tones in my ear. I sat next to Theo who again seemed not to participate. The song was unfamiliar, therefore I listened. My guess was that they were singing in a tribal language.

In that language, the Colonel prayed before another song was sung. I joined in on:

Blessed Assurance
Jesus is Mine
Oh what a Foretaste
of Glory Divine

Colonel asked Theo to pray. He did and quite well, I must add. The Colonel prayed asking the Lord to grant Mr. & Mrs. Ekuban safe passage to Ghana. Today, they are leaving New Jersey. Colonel Napoleon prayed for Fred (Amarkai), and then I heard the words "Brother Will".

He asked the Lord to bless me and my family... to get into... and take over... and help me understand his omnipotence. AMEN to that! Melody had fallen to her knees praying. The benediction was then offered by the Colonel. For the first time, Colonel was wearing traditional African wear.

The Ghanaians refer to his outfit as an *Up and Down*. There were pants (down) and a top (up) reaching near his knees. The colors in his *Up and Down* were light blue with a multicolored design throughout the outfit. The Colonel acknowledged the presence of Amarkai and me... expressing surprise that we had come. In Ghana, it is now 7 a.m. That means that the time in New Jersey is 3 a.m.

Since our arrival, we had been trying to get an adapter, so we could charge the camcorder batteries. Voltage in the U.S., as you well know, is 110. Here we need 220. Colonel promises to try to find an adapter before we visit the Botanical Gardens.

It was still early, and I went to my room to sit on the bed. The door was open and Nica entered the room. In her quiet submissive voice, she asked... "May I dress your bed?" Hurriedly, I agreed to her request... OH! FOR THE GOOD OLD WAYS.

BOTANICAL GARDENS

Amarkai and the young bloods went jogging. Amarkai returned drenched in sweat. The others seemed less sweaty. I kidded Amarkai telling him that the young bloods had tired him out. His reply was that they had quit on him leaving him to run most of the distance alone.

While Nica was dressing the bed, Amarkai challenged each of the young bloods to a game of table tennis... they don't use the term ping pong. Amarkai seemed to be winning. Although my game is a bit rusty, I challenged Amarkai. No excuses, but you can probably guess the results.

Amarkai had to do the last of his obeisance. Colonel had found an electrician who brought an adapter I could use to charge the batteries. Just as soon as he plugged it in, someone in the house found the household adapter. I asked the Colonel how much money I should give the electrician for coming to the house."200 cedis is enough" the Colonel said. I only had a 500 cedi bill. To use the Colonel's words, "the electrician is very lucky today". Roughly 500 cedis is about $1.25. Can you imagine that? So little money for a visit by an electrician.

I charged the batteries to the camcorder and also charged my electric shaver. For awhile, it appeared that I would have to resort to Gillette... or something else. In the living room, the young ones were watching 'Crocodile Dundee'. I went out on the porch and read some of the camcorder instruction book. If having a little knowledge of something makes one dangerous, then by reading the manual, I must be that.

Camcorders were completely new to me. I took video of Adolph, Akos, and others pounding fufu. Someone grabbed the camcorder and took me attempting to pound fufu. As I pounded, Akos re-spread the plantain and cassava. She was justifiably concerned for her fingers as I pounded. There was laughter at my pounding but concern for her fingers.

Theo, Will, Adolph, and Akos   Will pounding fufu
(Akos careful of fingers)

Mamiefia bows head to avoid camera - Ursula hid

Everybody (not quite) was getting on the video and giving their names. I learned that Mama Panyin's name is Mary Davidson... nothing Ghanaian about that name. Theo, Fulash, Mamiefia (Anita) and Ursula were all there.

Before arriving in Ghana, Amarkai told me about certain traditions, e.g., if someone takes you someplace that is unplanned, you are expected to pay their expenses. No problem... I am all prepared... I think. Colonel had suggested that we visit the Botanical Gardens. I expected to pay his expenses. When it was time to go, his wife and her friend, Nica, got into the car. Oh well! We are now on our way to Aburi, Ghana... home of the Botanical Gardens.

The town of Aburi is located up in the Aburi Mountains which are the highest mountains in Ghana. Aburi is about 20 kilometers east of Accra. On the way, we passed the Peduase Lodge. When the head of state wants to rest, one of the places he is likely to go is the Peduase Lodge. It must be similar to Camp David in the United States.

To enter the gardens, I had to pay in order to take in the camcorder. Fortunately, the security guard gave me a break. He allowed me to pay 1000 cedis for the camcorder instead of the posted amount of 2000 cedis. For an entry fee, each person was charged 2,500 cedis. My total bill came to 10,000 cedis which was approximately $11. Hey! That wasn't bad... No complaints.

Colonel, Nica, friends
near gardens

Sign to Botanical Gardens

Gift Shop   Drummers outside gift shop

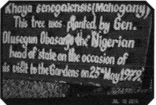

Where silk tree is planted   Mahogany tree
planted at this spot

There was an African Gift Shop at the entrance to the gardens. Drummers were playing outside the shop. Inside the trees and grass seemed immense. Earlier, at North Legon, I had videotaped the young bloods pounding fu fu (practice). My video expectations, at the Botanical Gardens, were high.

I had been told that the trees and flowers would present a very beautiful sight. We saw trees that had been planted by dignitaries from around the world... One of which was Nelson Mandela current president of the Union of South Africa. I was not disappointed. The visual display at the Botanical Gardens was unforgettable. There was a silk cotton tree (eiba pentandra (bombacaceri)) planted in 1924 by Sir Gordon Guggisberg. Additionally, there were banana trees, coco, and breadfruit trees.

A mahogany (khaya senegalensis) tree was planted by General Olusegun Obasanjo a Nigerian head of state on 25 March 1979.

That same day, General F. W. Akuffo. Ghana's head of state, accompanied by the Nigerian head of state, also planted a mahogany tree. Approximately one month later, General Akuffo would be ousted in a coup d'état before he was executed in a firing squad.

Flight Lieutenant J. J. Rawlings, Ghana's head of state, visited the Botanical Gardens in celebration of the Aburi Odwiri Festival 19 October 1990. He planted an araucaria cunninghamii (araucoriaceae) tree. The tree is commonly known as a hoop pine tree.

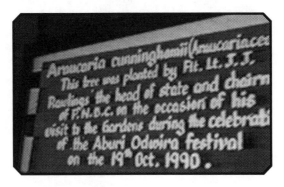

Colonel Napoleon and his wife attempted to explain to me the air force junior officer hierarchy. What I understood was in ascending order there is pilot, flying officer, flight lieutenant, squadron leader, wing commander, group captain, and air commandant. Several of Ghana's coups were instigated by the Junior Officers led by Flight Lieutenant Jerry John Rawlings.

Garden path surrounded by royal palm trees

A garden view

Colonel and Sarah look at coco tree. Coco was once Ghana's major export

A breadfruit tree (Artocarpus altilis) is said to be a potato like substance

Will pumping water at gardens

A little girl brings water for Will to fill up

At a small water pump, I pumped water while the Colonel shot the video. It seems that I was pumping so well that a young girl, about 4 or 5 years old, drug a bucket over to me to fill up with water while her parents sat on the ground laughing. This is where many local (Aburi area) people get their water.

Will, Nica, and Sarah checking out the helicopter

The Botanical Gardens were beautiful and quite large. There was so much to see. So many royal palm trees had been planted. I saw a few Indians there who also seemed to be enjoying themselves. Off to the side was an old U. S. helicopter which according to the colonel had been sent to the Congo years ago but brought to the gardens. Inside the helicopter was a catapult (sling shot).

We had to leave, but there was so much more to see. On our way home, Sarah (Christian name of the Colonel's wife) wanted some bananas. Looking as we drove down the road, we saw no one selling bananas. There was one purchase... a pounding stick. Trust me... These Ghanaians really have a love affair with fufu.

At home, everyone except Amarkai had eaten. He claims to have been waiting for me. Mistakenly, I think the meal is kenkey, but Amarkai quickly corrects me. Of course, he gives me a culinary history lesson. At one time, fufu was primarily cooked and eaten by the Akan of central Ghana, but now many other tribes also enjoy the meal.

Generally, a glass of water is taken with the meal. The water is to wash down the fufu. Popularly, fufu is eaten with the fingers. With the meal, there is a finger bowl available to wash your hands.

Additionally, there are napkins and a bar of soap to eliminate the smell from your hands.

That night we had orange slices for dessert.. Amarkai was quick to point out that the orange looked somewhat different in color from American oranges since it had not been processed. The soup poured over the fufu had beef, fish, and crabs in it.

In the living room, everyone seemed to be enjoying an Olympic basketball game featuring America's Dream Team. Amarkai mentioned to them that I 'hooped'. Modestly, I added... and quite well. We all laughed.

Everyone seems comfortable and free around me now. It seems that the novelty is wearing off. In the living room, that night, Adolph, who aspires to be a lawyer, introduced a political discussion. To let me know that he was up on U.S. politics, Adolph proudly declared himself to have been a Ronald Reagan supporter and just as proudly proclaimed himself to now be a Bush man, i.e., George.

Further elucidating his sentiments, Adolph made it crystal clear that "George was right in dealing with Sadaam and Noriega (the drug dealer)". I questioned him at length on that and the next morning so did Amarkai. Hopefully, it is not too late... Reagan and Bush?... Really!

NEGOTIATION 101

One bargains then buys
In the country of Ghana
It is cultural

Sunday, August 9 - Although I had forgotten to pack a tie... no excuse... I did expect to get another invitation, from the Colonel, to attend church. He did not invite me, but he did announce that he was going to church. For whatever reason, I think that he was the only one, in the house, who went to church today.

After a breakfast of eggs, potatoes, lettuce, Amarkai and I drove into Accra. As he drove, he was pouting because the breakfast was not what he had wanted. According to Amarkai, the breakfasts we had been eating were not real African meals. Although I made no requests, the breakfast choices were made because of me. I tried to comfort him, but Little Amarkai... him not happy.

We drove to the Old Polo Grounds where Kwame Nkrumah's body was to be exhibited. Because Nkrumah had done so much for the country, his body was to be exhumed and re-buried at the Old Polo Grounds. Today his body was not displayed, but eventually, it will be, so we are told.

The Old Polo Grounds, so named because this is where the good British gentlemen once played polo when Ghana was a colony, is located across the street from the parliament house where the Ghana legislators enact laws.

I guess it shows. To get into the Nkrumah Museum, foreigners must pay 2,500 cedis. Ghanaians pay 500 cedis. Amarkai was told that I wanted to see Chairman Rawlings about this discriminatory display.

Quickly, Amarkai equated this situation with his having to pay more money, than a U.S. citizen, to attend school in the United States. I told him... *America... Love it or leave it.* We both laughed at that.

The museum had recently opened. Fred and I agreed to come back to the museum at a later date when there is more on display. From there, we drove to the Christiansborg Castle which I gather is similar to the White House. As we approached, the military guards had their weapons pointed, toward us, from their stations although their fingers were not on the triggers.

A man, in civilian clothing, coolly watched us as we neared where he was standing. It appeared that he was in charge. I watched and listened as he and Amarkai talked. He didn't appear to have a weapon, and he calmly told Amarkai that we could neither photograph nor visit the castle without a permit. One doesn't easily get a permit.

The castle which is located in Osu was first used as a trading post for gold and ivory, but later under Danish control, it was used to transport human slaves. Another stop was at the Accra North Post Office. To me, it seemed that the only reason the building was open was to allow people to make phone calls... primarily trans-Atlantic calls. Perhaps other business was conducted there, but I don't know for certain.

When I announced that I wanted to make a collect call, the woman in charge thought for a moment before stating "O.K. I will let you use my phone". Immediately, Amarkai knew that her response meant money. Before agreeing, the two of us went into a phone booth to confer. We came up with 500 cedis between us.

After telling the woman that we would make the calls, Amarkai went into one booth, and I went into another to call Wes. On leaving the phone office, Amarkai extended his hand as if to shake the woman's hand. Had you looked closely, you would have seen him *slip* the money to her.

The protocol was obviously to pay for the call on the Ghana end. I veered from that direction and hence the payment of the *bribe.* While driving along, we saw Rasheed Kawawa one of Amarkai's Muslim buddies. He was U.S. hip... "Hey soul brother. You stay in Ghana. I look out for you". I think he hangs with the brothers when they come back home... visiting Ghana.

Our final visit today would be to the Accra Arts Center where they have a lot of things for sale. I settled on a xylophone and a few head carvings. The xylophone was made from wooden strips, on top, and several globe like calabash attached beneath each strip. By hitting the wooden strips from the top and impacting the calabash, musical sounds are created. I plan to give the xylophone to Wes.

I hampered Amarkai's negotiations for the price of the xylophone. The vendor began at 35,000 cedis. Amarkai countered with 25,000 cedis before the vendor said 30,000. When Amarkai's eyes shot toward me, I thought that he was asking for input. After a little thought, I offered 27,000 cedis. Turning toward me, Amarkai said "you blew". Everyone laughed... the vendors... Amarkai... and everybody else.

Trying to undo my blunder, I said 25,000. It was too late. We agreed on a price of 26,000 cedis. My ignorance had cost me 1,000 cedis. The vendor was a Muslim brother. He seemed O.K., but one of his partners was adamant and wouldn't accept no as he tried to sell his goods.

He and some of the others had a high powered sales approach. It became incumbent upon me to be even more adamant in my refusal than he was in his insistence. I was sincere when I told him that I would return.

Although I wasn't buying any, in another section of the arts center, we checked out some kente cloth. In the course of our conversation, the vendor surmised that I was living in the U.S. To gain favor, he said "My man Leonard Jeffries will be here soon". It seems that this was the time of year when Dr. Jeffries, head of the African Studies Department at CCNY, brings a group to Ghana.

I thought we were on our way home, but we stopped at Sister Nana's house. They had just come back from church... Praise the Lord. In Ghana, they church at least as much as some in the U. S.

Ka-bob is very spicy but delicious and quite similar to the shish Ka-bob. The first time I met Sister Nana, she treated me to a Ghana Ka-bob. Today's treat, although unexpected, was well appreciated.

Later that evening, we returned home and ate fufu. The eating of that meal was videotaped. I hope that it will be clear. Rev. Neequaye had just finished a bowl of fufu. Perhaps we can compare Ghanaian ministers to fufu with Black Baptist ministers from the U.S. to fried chicken.

Amarkai had to leave the house again. He asked Rev. Neequaye if he needed a ride home. Reverend replied that he would talk it over with the Lord. Fred Ekuban, who I met a few days ago, came by, and we talked awhile before he left. Joy offered to wash and iron my dirty clothes, but I suggested that we wait. He asked if I wanted juice to which I responded... Yes please. Ten to fifteen minutes passed, and Joy had not returned with the juice. For him, that was totally out of character.

From my bedroom, I walked toward the living room and heard what reminded me of 'church like' voices. Then I heard singing. Surmising that they were having church again, I quietly tip toed back to my room.

Amarkai came back in the house and told me that the rev had asked him for a ride home. Rev must have had his talk with the Lord because Amarkai was gone again. He did leave me some *Tiger Nuts*. No one seems to know what they are. The outside of the shell resembles tiger skin. To eat them, you are supposed to chew without swallowing anything... but the juice. Many claim that the nut is an aphrodisiac.

Rev must have been conducting the church services that delayed Joy, because when Amarkai left to take him home, Joy came back with the juice. The juice tasted good, and it was very cold.

Mirikoda... I am going to sleep

THE COMPLIMENTS

Monday, August 10 - Nica came by my room early this morning. She was collecting clothes that needed to be washed and ironed. As we left the house, Adolph paid me the ultimate compliment, i.e., "Today you look like an African". I don't know if it was due to my clothes, but I was wearing blue striped pants with a matching shirt worn outside my pants. On my feet, I wore brown sandals. In any event, I enjoyed the compliment.

Amarkai's comment was that I had been wearing shorts down town, and Africans don't ordinarily do that. He was obviously forgetting that it was he who suggested that I wear shorts, and he too was wearing shorts... downtown.

We were up early today, i.e., 6:30 a.m., primarily because we had to drive Joy, Theo and Fulash to the Atchimota School. Adolph and Melody also rode with us. Melody's ride was to the market, whereas Adolph was going to go wherever we went. The vendors were out early. It seems that they never sleep.

Just as frequently, we also see beggars every day. Some of the beggars are Fulanese people. Fulanese are the offspring of the mixture of the Berbers and Negroes... according to the white scholars. Negroes?,,, Hmm... Where have I heard that term before?

One of today's stops is to the office of the Ekuban's paper supply business. Pat Osei, the secretary, brought me *a spot of tea* while sharing with me her fondness for *hip hop music*. I took a few pictures of Pat and others in the office.

The phone rang, and I noticed how formally Pat queried the caller. "Can you declare your identity"? I think that is British for... *Who's calling?* Mr. Ekuban also called while I was at the office. Pat chided him for not even sending a postcard. Before hanging up, he extended greetings to me.

We had to find out whether or not the mirror on the Volkswagen was going to be fixed. It seems that the mirror has to be ordered. That means it will take at least 3 months to get it unless the order is air mailed, then it will take only one month. In any event, it seems that Theo will have to face up to the likelihood of facing his mother before the car has been completely repaired.

The mechanic, who took off the door to check the mirror, expected a few coins. When he was almost finished, a few others gathered around. They too wanted to share in the *booty*. Amarkai gave the mechanic, who did the work, 500 cedis. We could hear the others asking for a cut. The mechanic, who did the work, seemed to have no difficulty in voicing his refusal to share. From there, we went to the American Embassy. This time, Amarkai wanted to get data on the protocol necessary to bring his brother to the U.S. as a student. The Ghanaian security guard told us that we needed passports to get into the embassy.

Amarkai asked him "Do you ask the white man for a passport?" There seemed to be a slight hesitation before answering, but he said... "yes". Amarkai said... "Fine, if you are consistent".

Amarkai showed his passport, and we learned that the staff was on lunch break. A Ghanaian woman, working for the embassy, happened to come out the door. Amarkai asked the guard if he could speak with her. The guard nodded yes.

Many of Amarkai's questions were answered by the woman. She was very cooperative. She thought that I was Ghanaian and the brother to whom Amarkai referred. Hey another compliment... two in the same day. Since we had some time before the embassy was to re-open, we decided to eat out. This is an absolute first.

As for food, in the area, the woman suggested an American fast food store... Papaye. If we were going there, she wanted a ride. Our plans were not to go there, so the woman, telling us that she would see us after lunch, walked off in another direction.

We didn't find another eating place and ended up at Papaye's anyway. Papaye's seems to be run by Syrians/Iranians or people close to that blood line. Adolph, Amarkai and I had 3 broasted chickens, which were not very tasty, cole slaw, french fries, and fanta (orange) minerals.

Since we ended up at Papaye's, we decided to take the woman at the embassy a chicken order. While still at the restaurant, a fellow walked over to our table. His name was Agrey-Fynn, and Amarkai had known him in New Jersey. The two of them talked, for awhile, before he left. I was told that Fynn is one of those good English names, and the Agrey-Fynn name resulted from Ghanaian and British intermarriage.

We ordered another round of orange drinks. When we were almost ready to leave, Agrey returned. He told Amarkai that he had a contact person for him if he were interested in buying land near Mr. & Mrs. Ekuban.

It was a short ride back to the embassy, and the guard let us in... without displaying our passports. Of course, Amarkai still had his. I didn't even have mine the first time.

Intentionally, we had left the woman's snack in the car. When the circumstances were told to her, she agreed to accept the snack. I went to the car to retrieve it and gave it to her. She thanked us... asked our names... and told us hers, i.e. Margaret.

Off to another section of the embassy, we marched. Amarkai got little satisfaction, and in a short while we left the embassy. Adolph had been very nice and helpful all day. When we had to leave the car, he lugged around my camera bag. Please don't forget his compliment earlier this morning about my *looking like an African.*

On the way home, we stopped at a British Airways office to get information concerning our return baggage. It seems that each person is allowed 2 free bags each of which can weigh 70 pounds. For all other bags, excluding carry on, a fee of $116 per bag will be charged.

Before heading for North Legon, there is one more stop. On the street, an artist was selling his paintings. When the car stopped, we got out and went to look at them. He said he was selling them for 15,000 cedis before going down to 14,000. After some negotiating, Amarkai offered to buy 2 for 20,000 cedis. The artist shook his head denoting... no.

"Let's get kicking" said Amarkai, and we walked away. After only a few steps, the artist called us back. This time, he was almost pleading. He mentioned that he was from Kumasi and would need some of his money to get home. Amarkai was in control and seemed to ponder a hard line approach by sticking to 20,000 cedis for two paintings before relinquishing somewhat and agreeing on 21,000 cedis. We split the charge. There is one picture for Amarkai and one for me. Amarkai chose the painting of two African children which left me with one painting of a beautiful African woman. My painting will be given to James and Bessie.

Painting of African woman

When we arrived at the house, Adolph carried in my camcorder bag as well as the two paintings. As I walked through the door of my room, I could see that Nica had finished washing and ironing my clothes. Additionally, they were neatly folded on the clothing shelves. The work was nothing short of professional. Hurrah for the *old ways*. You know what I am talking about... *Natural Law... God's Law*. Don't become upset now.

In a talk with Fred Ekuban, he said that there was a herbalist in Ghana claiming to have a cure for AIDS. Whenever he was asked to meet with medical people to discuss his claims, he would fail to show up. While watching tonight's news, there was a report that another such meeting had been scheduled... Again the Ghanaian herbalist did not show up.

After a short delay, tomorrow, the Ekubans are scheduled to return home. That day promises to be Theo's *moment of truth*.

OSAGYEFO

Tuesday, August 11 - Last night, Amarkai must have been very tired because he went to bed about 7 p.m. This morning, about 3 a.m., Amarkai woke me up ranting some gibberish about the camcorder instruction book and wanting to talk. I asked, demanded, and finally pleaded for him to leave me alone. Unsuccessfully, I tried to go back to sleep.

It was early morning, and I got a bit more <u>interrupted</u> sleep. At 7 a.m., I was up for the day. Because of his harassment, this morning, I asked Amarkai *what was on his alleged mind*. His response was "You wouldn't understand... It's a Black thing". My laughter was immediate for now he was *stealing my thunder*.

After leaving home, our first stop was to a black market money exchange. Today's rate allows us to exchange one U.S. dollar for 450 cedis. Afterwards, we went back to the Kwame Nkrumah Museum at the Old Polo Grounds. After some small talk, the ticket seller, a woman, charged me as a Ghanaian (500 cedis) vs. 2,500 cedis for non citizens. Of course, *the bribe* cost me another 200 cedis.

The British played polo at this site, and additionally, on June 3, 1957, Kwame Nkrumah, Ghana's first head of state, delivered the Independence Day speech. Inside the museum, there were two female tour guides. They wore clothing that was primarily western. One wore her hair short and cropped *natural*. Her top was styled like a short sleeve V Neck sweater. The top was adorned with blue and black diagonal stripes. Her skirt was white.

Our guide, Abena, had straight black hair. She too wore a skirt and blouse, but her blouse was multicolored, and her skirt was black. Abena was very personable and seemed to enjoy her job.

Abena enlightening Will

There were many photos, audio cassettes and documents of Kwame Nkrumah and others... before, during and after his exile. Among the African heads of state visiting Nkrumah after he was elected president in 1960 were Patrice Lumumba, Prime Minister of the Republic of the Congo, and Kenneth Kaunda, Zambia's head of state.

In 1966, there was a coup and Nkrumah's government was overthrown. Nkrumah fled to Guinea. Sekou Toure was the president of the Republic of Guinea at that time. President Toure had so much respect for Kwame Nkrumah and his Pan-African ideals, that he offered to step down from his position in favor of Nkrumah. Nkrumah felt that Toure's gesture was too great an offer, but accepted Toure naming him co-president of Guinea.

In the 1966, 1967 time frame, a group of Ghanaians left Ghana and joined Nkrumah in Guinea. Kwame Nkrumah died in 1972, and his body was returned to his village, Nzima, in Ghana. When the body was returned, a *traditional man*, from Nkrumah's village, poured libation thanking the gods for the safe return of his body to Ghana.

Many heads of state, from around the world, paid their final respects at the funeral of Kwame Nkrumah. Among them were Fidel Castro of Cuba. An Akan name of respect, *Osagyefu... fighter for the rights of his people*, was the name by which many Ghanaians referred to Kwame Nkrumah.

When Nkrumah was overthrown, a statue of him was knocked down. Ghana Generals, Ankrah and Kotoka, were credited with masterminding the coup d'état. Since then the U. S. has admitted to a role in the coup. At this time, there seems to be an Nkrumah renaissance in Ghana. Outside the museum, the statue has been put up again.

One of Nkrumah's favorite quotes was "Forward Ever, Backward Never". Looking at the statue, you can see Nkrumah's finger pointing forward toward the parliament house.

To the rear of the statue is a marble like structure. The structure depicts a giant tree, with roots, that has been cut short. Actually, the tree represents a great man, Kwame Nkrumah, whose plans for Africa have not been fulfilled.

Statue of Kwame Nkrumah pointing toward the Parliament House

There are many designs on the marble like structure. Some of the designs are Ghanaian, e.g., *Linguist Staff and the Sankofa Bird.* The Sankofa bird is represented by a bird with its head turned toward an egg on its back. Abena said that sankofa means *"Go back to the past".* Literally Sankofa means "Return and take it". It is no taboo to return and fetch it when you forget. You can always undo your mistakes.

| Sankofa bird on marble structure | Linguists commemorating a death |

Other designs on the structure are more representative of Africa generally to point up Nkrumah's strong Pan-African penchant. We are told that Nkrumah's body has been embalmed and rests in the burial chamber at the museum. Many people leave wreaths in the area where Nkrumah is buried.

The area surrounding the museum is beautiful replete with water spouting from the water fountains. In the water are statues of African linguists blowing bull horns. Signaling that the horns are being blown, you can see water running from the bull horns. To commemorate a great person's death, the linguists blow the bull horns and create musical sounds.

Will watching the linguist blow his horn

Ghanaians have a saying "With water there is life". Nkrumah's body is dead, but the water suggests that his ideals live on. On visiting the museum, world dignitaries have sometimes planted trees. When Nkrumah was in Guinea, it was said that he would often rest under a mango tree. In November 1991, Nelson Mandela, President of the African National Congress, planted a mango tree. The seed of the tree was said to be from the mango tree in Guinea where Dr. Kwame Nkrumah often rested.

Sign is near mango tree planted by Nelson Mandela

Near the statue of Nkrumah, I met Adjoa who Amarkai dubbed "The African Child". To refer to her as beautiful would be an inordinate understatement,... but she was beautiful. Adjoa's skin was very smooth and a deep ebony color. Her hair was neatly braided, and she wore an up and down outfit where the skirt was a mid blue. The up (top) had a kente design surrounded by a blue color identical to the color of her skirt.

Adjoa (The African child) and Will

We videotaped many scenes. The tour guide was excellent, and so was Amarkai. I learned a lot.

Just entering the museum caused me to sense that I was at the Old Polo Grounds, on June 3, 1957, awaiting Nkrumah's speech. It was almost as though I could hear the beating of the talking drums, and elders urging Kwame Nkrumah (Osagyefu) to deliver the Independence Day speech...*Casa... Casa... Casa.*

With thundering applause interrupting many of his words, my ears were ringing with Osagyefu's words declaring Ghana's independence:

"We are going to demonstrate to the world... to the other nations... young as we are, we are planting our own foundation. As I said in the assembly just a few minutes ago, I made a point that we are going to strictly declare our own African personality identity. That is the only way we can show the world that we are politically over."

"But today, may I call upon you all, and on this great day, let us all remember that nothing in the world can be done unless it has the proportional support of God. We have done the battle, and we again re-dedicate ourselves... not delaying the struggle to emancipate other countries in Africa. Our independence is minimally linked up with total liberation of the African continent."

"Let us now... fellow Ghanaians... let us now... ask for God bless... and for only two seconds in your thousands and millions... I want to ask you to pause only for one minute and give thanks to almighty God for having led us through obstacles, difficulties, imprisonment, hardship and suffering to our protest to the end of our trouble today. One minute silence.......................... Ghana is free forever." And here I would like the band to play the Ghana National Anthem.

Leaving the museum area, I was stopped by a man behaving as though he was the person in charge. I think the woman who sold me the entry ticket works for him. His question to me was "Are you Ghanaian?"

I don't know whether or not the woman had mentioned me to him. My answer to him was... *Yes. I was born over here but raised over there.* He seemed to be puzzled by that answer, but I continued to walk through the exit gate. He too was interested in a *bribe.*

NO BRIBE

Since we were nearby, our next stop was the Parliament House where the legislative body meets. Amarkai's cousin, Tawiah Yoyowah, works in the Vetting Department located in that building. He is a lawyer who once lived in Cuba. Tawiah went to Cuba under a government sponsored program and studied Economic Crime.

As a youngster, he was referred to as Arafat. His Christian name *had been* Emanuel, but he dropped that name... preferring his own African name. Tawiah is slight of build and has long had the reputation of a radical.

As we leave Tawiah's office, Amarkai hands him a $100 bill. Obviously, he is still doing his obeisance. I think Tawiah directed one of the security people to show us the legislative chambers. That person seemed muscular, business like, and probably able to take care of most physical threats.

Taking pictures in the legislative chambers is absolutely taboo, but the security man allowed us to do so. Ghana has had three republics, and the chambers are being expanded to accommodate 200 parliamentarians in anticipation of the fourth republic. My suspicions are that not many people, non Ghanaians in particular, have ever been able to videotape scenes from the legislative chambers.

Will in the parliament house

After our tour, we thanked the security person (policeman), and thinking that he expected a bribe, we tried to give him money. Putting his hands over his heart, he bowed graciously, nodded no, and accepted our gratitude as we left the chambers. This was an absolute first... a mind blower. No bribe was paid, and none was expected. The obligatory bribe was absolutely refused.

Ghana's Coat of arms outside parliament house

Supreme court building

TRUTH DEFERRED

Outside the Parliament House, the parking area was relatively empty. Amarkai tells me that when the legislature is in session, there may be 50 to 100 cars in that area. The Parliament House was built prior to the time Ghana gained its independence. Looking up on the side of the building, you can see Ghana's coat of arms. Near the Parliament House is the Supreme Court building. Disputes that were once settled tribally are now, I assume, settled in the Supreme Court.

Walking to the car, we passed a female hawker carrying her goods in a basket on her head. Some young children... probably on their way home from school... saw Amarkai and thought he was from the TV station. They clowned around, making faces and laughing while I stood to the rear telling another hawker that I didn't want anything.

We stopped at the Art Center to look at some benches and kente cloth. As we parked, the persistent Muslim brother was at the car. Fortunately, we were able to get by him without too much pressure. Abdul Raheem is the name of the brother trying to find something that we like.

It is uncertain as to whether or not the bench parts will fit into a suitcase. After a cursory measurement of my suitcase tonight, I will have a better idea. Should it fit, I will probably buy it tomorrow.

Since we are running late, we hurry from the Arts Center. The Ekubans are scheduled to land about 6:37 p.m. Instead of going home, we head for Kotoka International Airport. On the way, we make a *pee stop* at the Safari Hotel alleged to be one of Ghana's better hotels.

Speaking of *pee stops*, it is not uncommon to see a man urinating on the streets... day or night. In many areas, the act is legal, but today I saw a sign that read "Do Not Urinate Here". For some of you, the act may be mitigated if I mention that I first heard of this practice associated with a European country, i.e., France. There seems to be a debate as to whether or not it still occurs in France.

Headed toward the airport, we see Colonel Napoleon driving the truck to the airport, and we follow him. Amarkai attempts to park in a VIP parking area. He gives the guard a story about having to pick up a dignitary. The guard is unimpressed. Someone, fortunately with more clout than the guard and known by Amarkai, comes to the gate.

This may have been pre-planned, but aloud I wonder whether or not the deceit was necessary. Amarkai's response was "I am home, and I know the tricks". So be it.

The plane had not yet landed, so we went inside to watch the landing. Awaiting the Ekubans was a large entourage... the minister, carpenter, secretary, Sister Nana, Apia (Sister Nana's brother in law) and a host of others. When leaving the terminal, Mrs. Ekuban came over to greet them. Although I had met Mr. Ekuban, I had not yet met Mrs. Ekuban.

When she approached me, I think she deducted that I was with Amarkai and hugged me warmly. Her reaction was reminiscent of Winnie Mandela when she met Betty Shabazz for the first time in New York City. She seemed to swing from not knowing who I was... to a sort of sudden recognition. Nana Sam, Mr. Ekuban, and I warmly shook hands.

Mrs. Ekuban, Rex, made it clear that she wanted to ride in her car. *Uh oh... my thoughts went to Theophilus.* Amarkai went to get it, from the VIP section, and Rex, Melody, Amarkai, and I headed home.

One of the things that Rex said, en route, was "Amarkai (Fred) is not a real Ghanaian. The real Ghanaians are back, and we will go many places". I think Amarkai's face reddened somewhat once again... well... not exactly red.

There was a brief *welcome home service* including a prayer. Praise The Lord. After which, soft drinks were served. Some of us went to eat. At the table, Colonel told Nana Sam (Sam) about *Theo's Incident.* Sam seemed not to be greatly concerned.

I picked up the wrong bowl. It was fufu and designated for Rex. Oops! When told of my faux pas, I quickly sat it down. My meal was rice, soup, meatballs and plantain. Rex finally came to eat, and one by one people left the table leaving only Rex and Colonel. I assumed he was prepared to present *Theo's Case.* In any event, I, with the others, left the room. FOR THE VERY FIRST TIME, SINCE I HAD BEEN IN GHANA, A WOMAN SAT AT THE DINNER TABLE WITH US.

Shortly, Rex called Amarkai to the back room to talk. Sam and I sat in the living room, and he outlined the week's itinerary, i.e., Tema, Tesano, Elmina, Cape Coast, etc. To me, it sounds great. Eagerly, I look forward to it. I told Amarkai that the real Ghanaians have come back home.

Wednesday, August 12 - This morning, I woke up early, so I was eager to badger Amarkai... You know... Pay back. Who knows whether or not my badgering worked? But... he did get out of bed. Most mornings, since our arrival, Amarkai has been jogging. Today proves not to be an exception.

From the compound, on the roadside, I saw two Ghanaians jogging. They were running on bare feet. Amarkai laced up his Reebocks. See what I mean about the foreigner (the ersatz Ghanaian)..

As for me, I shower, shave, and mete out the cedis that I owe Amarkai from yesterday's money exchange. When Amarkai went out to jog, I began to read 'In the Fog of the Season's End' by the South African writer Alex LaGuma. The battery from my camcorder had been charging for awhile, so I went to the hallway to unplug it. While in the hallway, I saw Rex who had just gotten out of bed. Cheerfully, Rex greeted me by saying *"Praise the Lord"*. Praise the Lord I responded and asked her how she was feeling. Her reply was "Fine".

A sweating panting Amarkai would soon return from his morning jog. To my surprise, he told me that Rex has not yet gotten the news about *Theo and the car* or *Theo cutting classes*. When Rex comes by the room, I exit. Perhaps this is the moment of truth.

For breakfast, we had eggs, potatoes, lettuce and avocados. Amarkai "him upset"... again... because "him" say breakfast made to satisfy me. *Poor little baby...* I told him that I make no special requests... I go with the flow.

I waited at the house while Amarkai drove the boys to school. When he returned, it was time to take Sam on some errands prior to Sam going to work. Most of the stops escape me. I didn't pay much attention. One stop was at Psycho Marx's place. Psycho and Sam do a lot of work together. My visit to the Botanical Gardens did not go unnoticed. Somebody from Psycho's clique had informed him of my visit there... a few days ago.

Sam seems to be a very easy going guy. He and the Colonel were trying to schedule some cultural trips for me. One possibility is the *Kumasi Festival* which does not begin until August 21. That trip, cultural in nature, may depend on my having the ability to change my departure date to August 23. In any event, I expect to see the Elmina and Cape Coast slave *castles*, on Friday or Saturday.

THE DEMON

Colonel Napoleon asked me to go with him since he was going to pray a demon out of a woman. I was pleased that he asked me to go and asked whether or not I could videotape something of that nature. Explaining that demons enjoy being filmed, the colonel suggested that I not film.

Citing an incident, the colonel recalled an instance when a demon was driven out from a woman under the scrutiny of film ... only to invade the body of the exorcist's wife. On hearing that story, I opined ... *of course we don't want that.*

We drove to the area where the *possessed one* lived. Before going to the home of the woman who was to be exorcised, we stopped at a beauty salon owned and operated by Ekua her close friend. Of course, I had the traditional *Akwaaba Welcome* when a glass of water was brought to me. The colonel refused. After a brief conversation, Ekua led us to see the one *possessed.*

She was introduced to me as *Comfort*, and she was a very attractive Ghanaian woman. One I wouldn't hesitate to refer to as sensuous. She wore a traditional garb that clung snugly to her shapely body. Although the garment revealed no flesh, there was not much doubt as to what it was hiding. Ekua returned to the beauty salon.

Our visit interrupted Comfort's meal. When Colonel saw that she was eating, he lamented at not having told her to fast before his arrival. Because she had not fasted, there was a limit to what the colonel would attempt today. He had her read some passages from the bible, and she read in her Fanti language.

The room was dimly lit, and I nodded a bit. I don't know if I was detected, but the colonel did flick on the lights. That pleased me because I thought that the lights would aid me in staying awake. **WRONG!!!** It wasn't even 3 p.m. yet, but I was nodding *big time* now. Why me?

After discussing several bible passages, Colonel remembered that he had to pick up the younger children from school. He asked Comfort to go get Ekua. When they both returned, Colonel explained that he would have to continue later tonight. In the interim, he would offer a prayer.

Colonel requested that Ekua put her hand on Comfort's stomach as he prayed *"Father make the demon idle inside this body ... Help this child ..."*. They were all standing. Perhaps I too should have stood, but there was no request. Consequently I sat. When the session concluded, we all said our good-byes. Colonel told them that he would see them later at one of the church meetings.

As we drove along, I asked the colonel whether or not Comfort was pregnant. His answer was negative, and he mentioned that Comfort had said that the demon attacks at the throat, moves to her breasts and ends up having sex with her. Colonel explained that instead of his putting his hand on Comfort's stomach, he had Ekua touch her because he knew that sometimes the demon uses lust in attempting to defeat an opponent.

NAMING CONVENTIONS

On our way to the school where we were to pick up the youngsters, we passed one of the local markets, and it was really busy. One of the secretaries from Sam's office lived nearby, and we saw her going home. As she and the colonel talked, I observed the sway of some of the trees. It seemed that they would sway in one direction, or the other, so much so until they would soon snap, but that did not happen.

Swaying tree

First we picked up the youngsters and then Nana Sam. From there, we headed home. Earlier this morning when we left home, Rex had announced that she was resting today. She was not going to work. When we returned home, she had some workers laying a rug. Even to a casual observer, it was obvious to all, Rex was in charge.

The pastor, who was not at the airport, was at the house. I suppose he was there to pay his respect to the Ekubans. Sam, Colonel, and Ursula gave me some information on Fanti naming conventions. Before deciding on a name, the father must agree to that name. If the father is dead, that responsibility falls to the father's brother.

The Fanti believe that man has three souls … the blood soul (moyga) lineal from the mother and synonymous with the clan … the spirit soul (ntoro) inherited from the father … the platonic soul (okra). To be certain that there is no mistake about the okra, a specific name is given to the child according to the day of the week that he/she was born. The day of the week in which you are born is pivotal. There could be many sons/daughters with the same first name. For purposes of distinction, the father would probably give a second name.

There are more than a few different tribes in Ghana. Each has its own naming convention. One can laugh at being asked if they speak African. What about asking if they speak Ghanaian? That question is just as ludicrous.

I continue to marvel at how beautiful some of the Ghanaian names are and enjoy hearing Ghanaians say those names. Then I am saddened at how many of them have English names and in some instances are more proud of their English names than their traditional names.

Fanti Names For the Day of the Week on Which You Were Born

	MALE	FEMALE
Monday (Adwadah)	Kojo	Adgoa
Tuesday (Abrandah)	Kwabina	Abena
Wednesday (Oohqwadah)	Kweku	Ekuwa
Thursday (Yawadah)	Yaw	Yaa
Friday (Ehfiahdah)	Kofi	Efua
Saturday (Minmindah)	Kwame	Ama
Sunday (Kwesiada)	Kwesi	Esi

An example of a naming convention within the Ga tribe follows: There could be an Amar family within the Laryea family. For example, there could be a first born son whose name would be Nii Amar. The second born son would be Nii Amarkai, and the third born son would be Nii Amala. Fred Winston Laryea, the Brit, is actually Nii Amarkai the second born son in the Laryea family.

After dinner, the family gravitated to the living room to watch the tellie. I wish I could duplicate Rex's voice with a pen, but Rex purred to me *"you should sit next to me"*. I did.

As we talked, she summoned JoJo (Theo). He answered *"yes ma'am"* but did not move. Again Rex called JoJo, and JoJo responded "yes ma'am". Sternly Rex said *"When I call you, you should come to the front where I can see you"*. Immediately JoJo came and stood in front of Rex.

Theo seems less apprehensive these days. Obviously Amarkai was successful in saving his behind.

TEMA

Thursday, August 13 - We were up early around 6:30a.m. For breakfast we had beans and some kind of meat ball. Amarkai felt better about this meal, and emphasized "**THIS IS AN AFRICAN MEAL**". Today Nana Sam drove us around in his truck. Sam's truck is a 1989 grey Suzuki pick-up truck. Our first stop is a travel agency. They are trying to get me confirmed for an August 23 departure. Amarkai may have to stay in Ghana a bit longer. London to Newark is o.k., but now I have to get from Accra to London.

Apia, Sister Nana's brother in law, is alleged to be connected to a prostitute ring. He told me he would fix me up with a light skinned woman and was persistent with his offer. I said no thanks as I thought about the impact of 'light skinned'. I wondered was that choice (light skinned) his perception of black men from America, or was that his own preference.

To look at material, we visited a boutique shop. The voice of the shop's proprietress sounded French to me, but Sam said she was Ashanti from Central Ghana. Tomorrow we are scheduled to look more.

Kwame Nkrumah was responsible for creating Tema an industrial center outside of Accra. There are steel mills, textile plants, oil refineries, etc. They seem to employ a lot of people, but things have slowed as the economy slowed. That sounds U. S. familiar. We went to an area where fishermen take their canoes out to fish. I was set to record when a young guy alerted me that photos were forbidden. He mentioned something about foreigners taking pictures and using the film commercially. Who is he calling a foreigner? Amarkai cited his Ghanaian citizenship and defiantly snapped a picture of me with the canoes in the background.

Nana Sam's elder brother, who works at or owns one of the Atlas plants there, told us there was strict security on taking pictures. Oops! Amarkai broke the law, and I verbally chastised him, a foreigner, for not being more respectful of OUR laws. We, Nana Sam, his brother, Amarkai, and I all laughed at that.

Will at Tema - fishermen in the background

Before we got to Tema, we stopped to eat at the Country Kitchen Restaurant. Both the food and restaurant were very nice. All of us had fufu. My sauce had bush meat in it. Bush meat is smoked meat from animals living in the bush... quite often a 'grass cutter'. I was told that the hair is burned from the bush animals. Later when I saw a man selling one on the road, I regretted having eaten the sauce. It was rough looking and reminded me of an aardvark

When we got home, our meal was jollof rice, plantain, and chicken. I didn't eat much since I was still full from the restaurant. Rex insisted that it would be there for breakfast tomorrow morning. Fine I said, since I felt my appetite would surely be better then.

After dinner, Sam had to take care of some business. Consequently, Sam, Rex, Amarkai, and I took a drive. Rex said it was a rough part of the town. I don't know if government control of the news explains it, but I have heard no mention of violent crime since I have been here. Fred Ekuban did mention that he had his pocket picked.

When we got home, we played back some of the videos we had taken. Some of the scenes were good, but there seemed to be a disconcerting sound emanating from the cassette. We surmised that it may have been noise from the wind.

A bigger concern was that the video came out in black and white. There was no color. By the way, Adolph addressed me as Uncle Will... a closer reference making me part of the extended family. While we were setting up the camera and TV, 'church' was going on in the living room.

Friday, August 14 - Today Amarkai is 'Driving Mrs. Ekuban'. The first stop was a clothing design shop run by Mawuli Kofi Okudzeto. When I was introduced to him, Amarkai quizzed me about the meaning of the name Kofi. Before I could respond (I knew the answer), Rex, in obvious support of me, responded that it means he was born on Friday.

In the states, some urban blacks might refer to the shop as 'Boughie' meaning for the have-nots prices are not thought 'friendly' (smile please). Amarkai and I bought some small gifts. There is no bargaining in Kofi's shop, but since Rex is a regular customer, she has earned a standing discount. Two shirts are selected by Rex, and she gives one to Amarkai and the other to me.

Although I was quite thankful, there was no change in my facial expression. Kofi commented on that, and Amarkai explained that he will never see more. We all laughed, but Amarkai's assessment was correct. MaMa who was also in the car was dropped off at the market to do grocery shopping. Later we stopped and bought some roasted plantain and peanuts.

When we drop Rex off at home, Amarkai has to pick up Mamefia and Ursula from school. They were glad to see us, but they wanted me to be the driver. Perhaps because I was visiting from the U. S., and that would be a good conversation piece.

We hadn't given up yet on seeing the Osu Castle. On the way home, we stopped at the Ghana Tourist Center to seek permission to visit the Castle. The Castle is Ghana's seat of government. It can be likened to Washington, D. C. in America. We were told that the Protocol Officer is located elsewhere, and that is who grants permission. Amarkai suggested that we forget it... I concurred.

At home, the Colonel invited me to go to church with him later that evening, and added that I would be able to take video. As much as I was eager to video tape church service, I declined his offer, because he expected to be there three to four hours.

Colonel asked me to play table tennis with him. I knew what he was talking about but was much more familiar with the ping pong synonym. We did not play an actual game, but we hit a series of volleys. Those few volleys demonstrated that the Colonel could play a bit, although he insisted that he had not played for twenty years.

Joy watched us for awhile. In his noticeably British manner intoned "You don't play table tennis very well". For his reference to my lack of game, I sarcastically said thanks a lot.

The Colonel and I must have continued for an hour or so. Finally, I begged off and went to take a shower. Ghana's heat is such that frequent showers are a necessity. By that time, Nana Sam had come home and invited me to go with him to deliver some plants to a friend in Tema. His friend is a retired military colonel.

When we arrived at the house, the opulence was quite evident. I was told that the house was once owned by an American diplomat. However, his friend was not home, so we did not go inside the house.

Tema's residential area is divided into numbered communities, e.g., Community 10. There are no signs identifying the communities, but Sam seems to know them very well. Sam mentioned that when Kaiser built its plant in Tema, the Americans had their own white community for its executives. Additionally, they had their own schools (white) patterned after U. S. school policies. A few years later, the community and schools were integrated.

All the foreign countries involved had an agreement with Ghana that after a prescribed time, all the work would be done by Africans. Sam was not certain, but he thought that prescribed time was ten to fifteen years. I forgot to ask who would be the owners.

I was advised, by Sam, that I should be ready at 6a.m. tomorrow to leave for Elmina one of the slave dungeons. We stopped for minerals (sodas). Adolph was with us, and I tried to pay for the minerals. Sam would not allow me. His rationalization was that he had asked me to come with him. Therefore the expenses were his.

I asked if it were permissible for me to take minerals to the others at home. The very 'laid back' Sam coolly asked "why do you wish to take minerals to the others". That more or less ended our discussion on that topic.

When we got home, Rex was eating. Mamiefia and Ursula brought our food from the kitchen to the table. We had karkro (ripe plantain), yam, soup, rice, and fried plantain for dessert. Karkro is prepared by adding flour, ginger, pepper and pounding the mixture in a mortar. It is then put in a skillet and fried in palm oil.

Several Ghanaian dishes are prepared by using a pounding stick in a mortar. The mortar is made from the trunk of a solid tree and chiseling out the middle.

After dinner, Rex and I sat down to talk. Rex said that she liked New York better than London, because she saw more people who looked like her. In London, she said Gambians and others seemed to look less like her. She asked about homelessness in America. When I told her that there was such a problem in the U. S., she opined that she thought it odd that there was also a homelessness problem in London but not in Ghana.

To explain why it is not a problem in Ghana, she used Ghana's extended family concept. I think her inference was that everybody in Ghana is thought of as family by at least one family other than their own. Consequently, one can depend on others in times of need, e.g., homelessness. Rex added that in London, there is a 'squatter problem'. One can leave home in the morning, and upon returning that evening, someone has moved into your house and boarded it up from inside.

Tonight's dessert treat is ice cream. It is home-made by a friend of Rex. I was in my bedroom when Akos, the house girl, came by and announced "your ice cream is ready". She did not have to repeat herself... I was on it.

CAPE COAST

One controversy
What slave traders named castle
Enslaved cried dungeon

Saturday, August 15 - I woke up at 4a.m. this morning. It might sound more exciting if I said it was in anticipation of seeing Cape Coast and Elmina, but the reality of it is that I had to go to the bathroom. After going back to bed, I again woke up at 5:40a.m. Amarkai came into the room inferring that I was late. Soon after that Colonel came by the room and announced that we would leave in ten minutes.

Shortly after six I was ready but everyone else was 'chillin'. We had a spot of tea (herbal cranberry) and some buttered bread. It must have been 6:30 or 6:45 before we left.

Our first stop was to be Cape Coast which is about 140 kilometers from Accra. Nana Sam says the distance is closer to 96 miles. I should mention that we prayed and sang before leaving. The way sam was driving, that prayer may have done the trick. Euphemistically, his driving speed was swift.

In Sam's truck, Sam and Amarkai sat in the front. Colonel and I were in the back. The way we took some of the bumps, one may have thought that we were riding wild stallions. On the way we passed a school that the government had set up for children from war torn Liberia. The route was scenic. In addition to newer building structures, we passed an old Dutch (I think) castle. In one village that we passed, they were having a festival. I was told that part of the festival will have young tribesmen set out on foot and capture a deer.

At times you can see fishermen in their canoes. After passing some prisoners working on the side of the road, I ask about Ghana's prison population. Fred informs me that one can be imprisoned for looking at someone in a position of authority. It seems that when the 'higher ups' want you, they can get you. Now where have I heard that before.

I mentioned the Emmit Till case where he was killed allegedly for whistling at a white woman. Additionally, I mentioned the case of the black man arrested for looking at a white woman. If memory serves me correctly, the charge was 'Reckless Eyeballing - Assault Without Contact'. All of us pondered over that for awhile. 'They' too seem to have gotten who they wanted.

When we arrived, there was an old sign describing our destination as the West African Historical Museum. Periodically one could see references to the Cape Coast Castle. The design may have been like castles I had seen in movies, but age had made the look not so elegant. The fort was built in the 1600s and was owned by different European countries including the Dutch and British. It was used extensively in the Atlantic slave trade. From Cape Coast, enslaved Africans were brought to the Americas and the Caribbean.

Cape Coast had been Ghana's capital city until 1864. Not even my initial view prompted me to refer to our destination as a castle. The site is on the Gulf of Guinea, and it's surrounded by small villages. In many of the villages, fishing is the main occupation. We could see fishermen sewing up their damaged nets in order to reuse them.

Sign at entry to dungeon

Fishermen sewing
nets for re-use

Chains used for heads of two captives

Inside there were actual displays of the muskets used by the slave traders, chains that held the heads of two captives together, pictures of the enslaved packed in dungeons. Additionally there were pictures of merchants bargaining for captives at the slave market and slave traders bargaining with their African collaborators. Prior to the slave trade, African tribes had used gold and to a lesser degree mahogany to trade with the Europeans. In exchange for the gold and mahogany, the tribes would receive clothing, blankets, spices, sugar, etc. The slave trade would prove to be far more lucrative than the gold trade.

There was literature suggesting that many of the captives had been captured in wars with other African tribes. In exchange for their captives, the African tribes were given guns, iron, cloth, beads (and items traded during the gold trade). The Ashanti tribe was one of the African tribes collaborating with the white slave traders in Ghana. For the conduct of the Ashanti and other collaborators, I search for no euphemisms. In my view, their conduct can collectively be likened to America's Benedict Arnold, Norway's Vidkun Quisling, and France's Vichy government... simply traitorous.

Benedict Arnold
Tribes aiding the slave traders
Birds of a feather

Fred (Amarkai?) at slave auction

The photo above shows Will in an empathetic mood for those sold at slave auctions. Printed beneath the slave sale information, in smaller print, "Also for sale at Eleven O'clock", to me, suggests that other items, such as food and materials, were sold at that particular market, but those sales were secondary to the sale of human flesh.

Another black man, visiting the museum from another country, turned to his son and mentioned Queen Nzinga, of Angola, who he said opposed the Portuguese slave trade for a number of years after collaborating with them.

America had a big demand for slave labor to pick cotton, tobacco, and sugar. Consequently many of the enslaved from Cape Coast were sent to the Americas. I asked one of the guides about the 'happy slave myth' that had been taught in my school. Colonel Napoleon in a stentorian voice shouted "THAT'S A LIE".

We were shown a male slave dungeon from where there were constant attempts to escape. Some succeeded. On a cannon ball, outside a dungeon cell, the 'disobedient' were made to stand until they collapsed. There was a 'condemned cell' where some were left to die. At various intervals, there was a mass burial.

Women had separate cells from the men. It seemed that at one time, you might find 1000 men and about 300 women captives in the dungeon.. The women were apparently used for the 'comfort' of the whites at the dungeon and at sea, but no reason was given for that particular ratio.

Will questioning the tour
guide on why the ratio
of men to women.

Dungeon view into the Gulf
of which would begin the
middle passage for the enslaved

The European governor had a little peep hole that he could use to pick out captured women who he would have brought to him in his quarters and then rape them. One of the nearby villages has a large population of mulatto/half caste people. They are descendents of those made pregnant by the whites and who did not make the voyage across the Atlantic.

When newly enslaved captives were brought to the dungeons, those designated as mulatto/half caste would bring anything that they thought would make the captives more comfortable... such as something that might lessen the pain of sleeping on the hard rocky dungeon floors. Empathetically, it must have recalled the experiences of their ancestors and them.

One of the buildings had a church on the top floor and a dungeon beneath. Visitors could see cannons pointed toward the Gulf of Guinea... apparently to challenge raids from pirates or other countries. One guide said there were some cannons pointed inland also to ward off attacks from villagers. Unfortunately, I did not see any of those. I picked up a few cannon balls. Although they had varying weights, some were the approximate weight of shot put balls (16 pounds) used in track field events.

At the dungeon, the attic was used to store goods that had been stolen from Ghana. The goods would be loaded on ships headed to their home ports. Some of the dungeons had limited light and space. The hole that provided light and air seemed inadequate for two or three people... not to mention an over packed dungeon. Phillip Quaque was from Cape Coast, and he is buried at the CapeCoast dungeon. He is the first Ghanaian to be trained and ordained as an Anglican pastor in London. In Cape Coast, he set up schools for the children of those referred to as half caste. He died in 1816.

Black captives ... passed a Gate of no Return
Somewhere on an African coast
Their African ways ... they had to 'unlearn'
Compelled by an unfriendly 'host'

A view of the Cape Coast Door of No Return

When the big ships arrived to take the enslaved human cargo far across the ocean to unknown cruelties, the women were marched from one side of the brick courtyard to join the men exiting their dungeons on the other side. They (men and women) exited to the ships through a gate/door which had come to be known as 'The Gate/Door Of No Return.

ELMINA

From Cape Coast, we headed for Elmina another of Ghana's old slave dungeons. Elmina was originally a trading settlement built by the Portuguese in the late fifteenth century but became integral to the Atlantic slave trade. In 1637, the Portuguese captured the fort from the Dutch. The dungeon was used heavily for the slave trade for more than 150 years.

Dutch slave traders sent many of their captives to Suriname which is on the northeast coast of South America. Many of the Portuguese captives were sent to the Caribbean Islands.

Pirate leaders were often sent to Elmina to die. Governors of the dungeon were said to be afraid to go near the captives. However they too had peepholes where they could identify and have an African woman brought to them for their sexual appetites.

The fear syndrome reminds me of my young days in Gary, Indiana. We lived in what was described as the rough part of town, where no white person in his/her right mind would be caught there after dark. That was what many white people said.

Remarkably, on a regular basis, white men could be found in our neighborhood long after dark looking for black prostitutes. Their presence was so prevalent that arriving in their cars reminded viewers of a ticker tape parade. Their car traffic was slow as they took in the sights. Even at night, one could see the anticipatory glee on their faces.

In looking for the prostitutes, they were not hesitant to exit cars, park their cars, and walk the streets. I suppose when that 'Sex Jones' comes to the surface, fear will somehow disappear... even if it is alleged to be present and strong.

In the dungeon, there is Prempeh's room. Prempeh I was an Asantehene of the Ashanti tribe. Asantehene is the title given to the monarch of the Ashanti people. There were many disputes between the British and Ashanti. Prempeh I was imprisoned by the British for four years.

Throughout the dungeon, one could see biblical scriptures on signs or walls. The church was upstairs in the 'castle', while the dungeon was underneath. One could say heaven was built upstairs in the 'castle' in deference to hell practiced below in the dungeons.

In the street, outside a dungeon, there was a cannonball, melded to the street, on which the disobedient were forced to stand. There were many similarities in how the Cape Coast and Elmina dungeons were laid out. Dungeons for men and women were on different sides of the street. Of course, the governor's peep holes were in both dungeons. Both had cannons facing the Gulf. There were churches, and the dungeon sizes seemed to be similar.

A surprising thing took place in Elmina. While touring the dungeons, we met two women from New Jersey. Their names are Carol Jones from Orange, New Jersey and Kim Singleton from Plainfield, New Jersey. When Kim and I detected that our surnames were identical, we did some cursory 'root checking'. It seems that her U. S. family originated in Georgia... mine in Mississippi.

Kim recognized Amarkai, because she had seen him in the New Jersey Institute of Technology (NJIT) area where he had attended school in Newark. She taught school nearby. All of us exchanged contact information and promised to keep in touch. It truly is a small world. Similar to my situation, they were living with a Ghanaian woman in a section called Roman Ridge.

Before leaving, Carol and Kim, who had traveled to different parts of Africa several times, shared an incident from Senegal. *On visiting, Goree Island, a slave dungeon, someone representing the Senegalese government made a special appeal to those whose ancestors may have been affected by places like Goree Island. According to them he apologized sincerely and in an unrestrained manner. The presentation was such that they both were moved to tears.*

On leaving the dungeons, there was a comment book to sign. Somebody from France commented "It was good". I didn't know how to interpret that. Another visitor commented "enjoyable" I wrote "historical". Perhaps I could have been more descript foregoing political correctness.

The Brit at Elmina

As we were leaving, Nana Sam bumped into an old friend who he had not seen in twenty years. Colonel, Amarkai, and I waited for Sam while he and his friend chatted for a few minutes. On the way home, we stopped and bought some tiger nuts and coconut. We were all hungry. That little snack did little or nothing to reduce that hunger.

At an Elmina restaurant, we all agreed to stop and get something to eat. They (excluding me) had fufu. I wanted to see what the Ghanaians could do with roasted chicken, rice, and cabbage (menu items). There was no disappointment. It was on time and remindful of the 'down home' meals, prepared by family and friends, that I ate and enjoyed as a youngster and as an adult. The taste was quite similar. The cooks obviously had 'soul'.

A well dressed Ghanaian man in his western attire sat at a restaurant table with a white woman. From a nearby table, a Ghanaian woman said to her date "white women are fine for Ghanaian men, but for Ghanaian women, you make white men a taboo". I did not hear his response.

Colonel lives in a village not too far from Elmina, so we stopped there for awhile. Still heading home, Sam did some roadside shopping, but we finally reached home about 6:30p.m. It is difficult to conceive, but as full as I was, we all ate again. We did play back video from Cape Coast and Elmina. I could see Nana Sam yawning. He said he was tired and excused himself.

Once again, my room has been cleaned by some of the ladies in the house. There is much to be said for 'well defined roles'... the men must be taken care of (enjoy). To quote a gentleman in Cape Coast, "Women are not ambitious like men. I didn't say this. He did. Kudos for the old ways (please smile at least). Although there is a house girl and house boy, the children (boys and girls) have duties they are expected to perform. They all do work around the house.

THE GANG (JOY)

I was also yawning and decided to go to my room. In a short period of time, Joy came to my room. We began to talk about the school system in Ghana. Ghana students, as USA students, begin with kindergarten. Unlike the U. S., after kindergarten, Ghanaian students take an exam. If the exam is failed, kindergarten is repeated.

Those who pass go into Class I. They are to spend six years in what is known as Prep II school. After the sixth year, a Common Entrance Exam is taken (no longer true). Now they begin secondary school which is called Form III (Junior Secondary School - for 3 years). If the exam is passed, one goes to Senior Secondary School for four years (Form IV).

Form V (Ordinary Level Exam). Then there is Form VI after which there is an Advanced Level Exam. Passing that makes one eligible for a university. Ghana has three universities... Cape Coast University, University of Science and Technology in Kumasi, and Ghana University in Accra.

One attends classes from September to December after which there is a Christmas and holiday break. The student returns in January, and classes are held until April when there is an Easter break. From April until June, there are classes after which there is a holiday until September.

Currently Joy is taking classes in physics, chemistry, mathematics, and additional mathematics. He wants to study medicine or computer science. Joy's full name is Joy Nana Ofesu Apiah Janko. Since he was born on Monday, Joy is also called Kojo. Finally Joy said he was going to learn, i.e. study/cram, but he would first have to iron his clothes for school. Prior to leaving, he played a gospel audio tape in the Twi language.

THE GANG (ADOLPH)

When Joy left, Adolph entered. He came in with his version of some hip-hop moves. Adolph laughed as I encouraged his dancing. I told him that I would show him some moves if he promised not to steal them.

Adolph asked me to sing the American National Anthem. I thought he was teasing, but he assured me that he was not. As a result, I sang it... sort of (smile). My performance caused me to request that Adolph sing Ghana's National Anthem. Although he had a tough act to follow,. Adolph very proudly sang the first stanza of the Ghana National Anthem - God Bless Our Homeland Ghana:

> *God bless our homeland Ghana*
> *And make our nation great and strong,*
> *Bold to defend forever*
> *The cause of Freedom and of Right ...*

Adolph was on his game, so he let me know that immediately after singing their anthem, they recite the national pledge:

> *I promise on my honour to be faithful and loyal to*
> *Ghana my Motherland. I pledge myself to the service*
> *of Ghana with all my strength and with all my heart.*
> *I promise to hold in high esteem our heritage, won*
> *for us through the blood and toil of our fathers; and*
> *I pledge myself in all things to uphold and defend the*
> *good name of Ghana.*
>
> *So help me God.*

As to education, Adolph has finished secondary school and has two more years before enrolling in a university. Tragically, in my view, he is another Reagan/Bush supporter... whew! After finishing his studies, Adolph wants to be a lawyer. He would not mind attending a university that is outside the country. Aware that Kwame Nkrumah attended a black university, he is not adverse to attending Lincoln University (Nkrumah's alma mater).

Since he was born on Wednesday, Adolph is a Kweku. Joy had drifted back into the room and actually joined in as Adolph sang the anthem but exited again saying he was going to learn.

THE GANG - THEOPHILUS (THEO)

Theo joined in. He has already entered Form V in secondary school. Not unlike Adolph, he is not opposed to attending Lincoln University in Pennsylvania, but he would welcome an opportunity to attend a good school in New York. Joy comes back in again and asks me to pray for him. Theo laughs and opines "Joy is sick".

Theo was born on Monday. According to him, he is Jojo in Fanti but Kojo in Akan. Like Joy and Adolph, they are familiar with many U.S. universities including the Ivy League schools.

Theo is quite relaxed and goes over to the xylophone to play some entertaining tunes. After an educational evening, we all decide to go to bed.

THE DISC JOCKEY

Sunday, August 16 - I woke up this morning with every intention of going to church. Amarkai says "you have to go to church today". My very firm reply dealt with two things that I definitely have to do, i.e. remain black and die. Mrs. Ekuban came by the room to announce that they were going to church. I asked at what time were they going. She replied 8 or 8:30. I said fine. Perhaps I do have to go to church today... chuckle.

We sat down for a breakfast that I found to be very enjoyable. The meal is called 'yaw ke gari' (my phonetic spelling), i.e. beans and gari which is made from cassava. After finishing my meal, I wanted and needed cold water. I am told that is par for the course. That meal is hot and spicy... at least.

Nana Sam invites me to go to church with him. He is Methodist, and Mrs. Ekuban is Pentecostal, so they generally go to different churches. Two of Amarkai's brothers, Sammie and Isaac, come by. Sammie and Amarkai leave the room.

It seems that Amarkai has a lot of brothers. I remember that Amarkai told me that the children of brothers are considered sisters and brothers... as are the children of sisters. They seem to cling tightly to that tradition. Children of brothers call their father's brother dad, and children of sisters call their mother's sister mama.

Isaac and I begin talking about telephones, fiber optics, basketball, soccer, tennis. We mention Magic Johnson, Michael Jordan, and Hakeem Olauwon, Manute Bol, et al. He said Amarkai played basketball in school. Later Amarkai embellished (I am sure) the story somewhat by claiming to have been a star.

That Sunday, Amarkai wanted to visit another church, but Sam drops the young bloods and me at Gethsemane Methodist Church. He plans to come back to that church after dropping off Amarkai. After a short wait to get into the church, an usher takes us to front row seats. My thoughts help me realize that the front rows are especially tough on nodding/sleeping. Perish the thought that I contemplated sleeping.

The church was under construction. I sense that will motivate a 'building fund' offering. At this time, the church has no windows. There is a canvas top supported by metallic/iron poles. The canvas seems to shade those who have no other protection from the sun. The building construction seems in its infancy.

The first offering, I dubbed the 'bargain' offering since the church gets two for one. There are two baskets. In one basket, worshipers can donate money to the building fund, and the other basket was for a church offering.

Visitors were asked to stand. I assumed that was what was occurring. Church service (prayers, offering, welcoming of visitors, etc.) is conducted in the Fanti language. I sat still until Joy corroborated what I was thinking. "This is your first" visit Joy said with his inimitable British voice. Joy was quick to add... "you must stand'. Oh... I responded adding that it is too late now. Adolph backed me up. Consequently I did not stand. That was the same pattern I had observed when visiting churches back in the USA. When visitors were acknowledged, I did not stand.

A speaker stood and eloquently appealed to members to give generously toward the building fund. As he spoke, I saw worshipers looking at the construction, so I assumed his talk was related to the building fund. Adolph or Joy confirmed that I was correct. There were a few other speakers, and my eye-lids became overburdened. Next on the agenda was 'the day of the week you were born' offering.

If possible, the atmosphere came alive. My eye-lids were less heavy. The choir and drummer were re-energized. Worshipers buzzed among themselves. A man in traditional garb (a very striking black and white kente draped across his shoulder) danced to the microphone and became sort of a disc jockey (DJ). As he clapped, danced, and chanted rhythmically, he beckoned/invited/sweet talked 'Monday people' (Kojo and Adjoa) to come forward. When coming forward, many of them performed dance patterns that seemed to express their individuality.

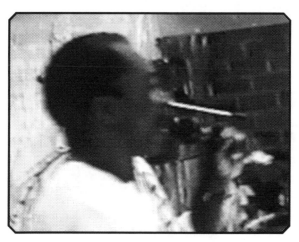

The DJ

Day of the week (born) offering

Offering dance

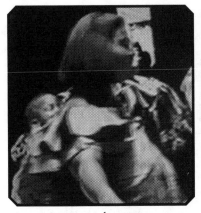

A young dancer on
his mom's back

Male in kente for
offering dance

offering dance

Some dancers would dance (intentionally) past the offering basket only to rhythmically maneuver back to the basket. Most of the dancers were women, but many men also danced.

The large majority of the worshipers were dressed traditionally. Bright colors were conspicuous. Kente was quite well represented. Outfits were yellow, brown, blue, purple, green, and various beautiful combinations. Others wore jeans, but were just as involved. I think the songs were sung in tribal languages, but some of the tunes I could recognize, e.g. Stand up for Jesus ye soldiers of the cross.

Sam came by where I was sitting and suggested that I 'march/dance' with Saturday people (Kwame). He said the minimum donation should be 2000 cedis and handed me the money. I returned it and told him that I would handle it I didn't mean to be offensive in my response, and I took no offense at his gesture. I am sure he meant no harm, but I believe people should give whatever they want or can afford to give.

I asked Sam if videotaping was permissible, and he answered "by all means". Joy wanted to tape, so I allowed him to do so. Adolph took over from Joy only to find that the tape had come to its end. When I put in another cassette, Adolph got busy again. Unfortunately, when Joy thought he was recording, he was not. I am uncertain as to the cause of the problem.

In any event, Sam and I ended up walking together. That was with the Friday (Kofi) group. Sam was not into dancing, so he positioned himself a distance from the dancers. I was disappointed, because I was ready to 'get down'... hee hee.

FULL STOMACH

From church, we did not immediately go back home. Despite that big breakfast I ate this morning, there was more food in store for me. Our clan congregated at Sister nana's house after church. Although everyone did not go to the same church, I think the large majority of those there had gone to some church. Today I learned that Sister Nana is Rex's youngest sister.

The first course of the meal was banku with soup. A next stop could be rice, then salad, and finally chicken/other meat. After the first course, I was done, but Rex asked me to come up for the next course. I told myself no way. She insisted that I come near her anyway... not to eat she said. I did, and of course, she ushered me to the salad line. My protests met deaf ears.

Some ate the traditional food with their fingers. Others used knives and forks. It seems that the gathering was due to Sister Nana's son, Nana Adu Gyamfi Dwimoh, who had his Catholic confirmation today. Today Nana Adu has taken on the English name Mark. He seems very happy and filled with energy.

Nana Adu (Mark) - Confirmation day

After the salad, someone brought over chicken and beef to sit in front of me. I tried to refuse, but Amarkai cajoled and begged. Somehow I finished that portion. This is only a partial account of my food intake. I will be remiss if I don't mention the soda, crackers, and doughnuts that were served when we first arrived at Sister Nana's house.

Rex feeding her face

The men and Rex began to talk about politics. Rex was not in the room long, but she made her point and left. No other women participated. Looking into the room where the other women sat, I thought I could see their chagrin at seeing Rex vying with the men.

The male conversation became hot and heavy. One contingent thought it was time for a civilian government in Ghana and Chairman Rawlings should step down. In order to minimize the likelihood of another military coup d'état, downsize the military. The colonel asked me if a military coup was likely in the United States. I opined that it had not happened, but I would hedge on concluding that it could not occur.

Most of the debates seemed to be started in Ga or an Akan language but would shift to English... perhaps for my benefit. If not in English, someone would lean over toward me and cooly tell me what was being said. In what seemed like the next instant, they would again get involved in the debate... hot and heavy.

Sam told me that it was time to go, but before going home, we had one more stop. This time Rex went with us, and the children remained. The next stop was an anniversary party, and they were, of course, serving food. I tried to decline. Rex came over, took me by the hand, and suggested that I take only a little. I took a little... a little salad, a little chicken, a little soda (chuckle). Without a doubt, I was full.

When we got home, I had visions of lying down. First Ursula came by my room, then Joy, Mamiefia, and more of Ursula's friends. Ursula confided in me that Joy was a bad boy, but she would not tell me why. Through the camcorder, we viewed scenes, i.e. church and Sister Nana's house, from the video taken today.

This evening, Ursula paid to me, what I think to be, a great compliment. She said "Uncle Will you are a Ghanaian. You cannot go back to America". I thought that was great and told her so.

My room was jumping. When Amarkai came by, he was surprised to see all the visitors there. Other than me, there were six people in the room before Adolph entered. Today Jojo, who sometimes seems aloof, took the camera and began taking video.

Finally, the troops left, and now I plan to get ready for bed. Oh! The young ones were shooting things at me in Fanti and laughing when I did not know how to respond. One last thing, Akos came by to tell me that dinner was ready. I said No... thank you. Tea... she asked? My response was No... thank you. Apple juice... she asked? I answered No... medasi.

TENSION IN THE TREES

Monday, August 17 - I got up and took a shower. Amarkai came in demanding to know whether or not I had showered and brushed my teeth. Of course not, I said. Those things I do once a year whether I need to or not. He told me some gibberish about the last person to talk back to him is still in the hospital. My response was... Now I am the last.

Amarkai drove the fellas to school. He will be coming back, so we can run a few errands. The camcorder is ready with two fully charged batteries. I write a few more post cards. While I am lulling around, Nica gently knocks on the door. Her knock is almost like a verbal whisper. When I say come in, she asks for my dirty clothes, and I tell her where they are. After collecting them, she smiles pleasantly and exits.

Should the norm continue, my clothes will be washed and ironed by the evening. The clothes will look as though they have been done in a professional laundry. I recognize that my response is trite, but MUCH CAN BE SAID FOR THE OLD ORDER. Halleujah! Praise God! Yesterday one of the men (Amarkai) said "this behavior is altered drastically when our women put on the jeans".

I heard a horn beeping at the gate. Amarkai must be back. In a few minutes, this African comes bopping into my room singing (?) "diddy diddy bom... jomp jomp - diddy diddy bom... jomp jomp". He swears he is U. S. hep.

We go to see Sam at work. Sam suggests that we wait around. Amarkai and I were supposed to look at some bikes, but Sam told us that he could get us a good deal at a FOREX bureau. That sounds good since we passed a bureau where the rate offered was 452 cedis for one U. S. dollar.

Quite a bit of time passed before Sam was ready. When he was ready, his car would not start. Sam took the battery out of his car and put it in the back of his truck. When the battery was checked, it was diagnosed as having a bad cell. The battery was left at the shop, and we went to a store that sold bikes. The manager, a female, seemed Lebanese, Iranian, or of a similar ethnic background.

The bike was priced at 45,500 cedis. The symbol for cedi is similar to an American 'cent sign' and precedes the numerical amount. When we opted to buy two, 500 cedis were shaved from the price of one bike. She accepted a $100 bill for the price of one bike.

From there we headed for Sam's favorite FOREX bureau, where they were exchanging 453 cedis for one U. S. dollar. I exchanged $700. For my $700, I received 317,100 cedis. I carried my stash around in a big BASF VHS bag. The bag is about 11 inches tall and close to 9 inches wide.. Hopefully, this is my last exchange, and I will have enough money for the remainder of the trip. Amarkai exchanged pounds for cedis.

When we went to pick up the girls from school, they had decided to walk, since it had taken us so long to get there. We met them as they were approaching the highway. That would have been a healthy walk. I should mention that we bought some 'Welcome to Ghana' posters. The posters cost 800 cedis apiece.

We went home to pick up Rex. One of the stops was to get the battery we dropped off. The shop was closed, but Sam called the manager, and since they were 'tight', he came back to open up so Sam could get the battery and put it in his car.

Amarkai, Rex, Adolph, and I left in the car. Rex stopped at a few places including Sister Nana's house where we had soup. There was another house where Rex had to stop, but we had trouble finding it. We finally found it. Rex and Amarkai went in. Adolph and I stayed in the car. Shortly, we were on our way home.

For dinner, we had yam, rice, and beans. Dessert was cut-up coconut over ice cream. After dinner, Rex invited me to walk around the compound with her. Believe me. This place is huge. Each time I think about it, the price in the states goes up. I think $400,000 is a very very conservative estimate.

As we walked around the compound, Rex talked about a lot of things, e.g. gardening, gardeners, plants, orchards,... children. Although a bit vague, I could tell that she was concerned about raising her children. I probably did not shed any insight, but I did comment that parenting is an extremely difficult and challenging job.

As we neared the gate, Sam drove up in his truck. We opened the gate for him. Back in the house, Amarkai had fallen asleep across the bed. With Rex's coaching, I went in to wake him up. He budged and smiled feebly, but I don't think he was pleased.

I went to my room to write about today's events. Joy came in to check the window. It was open. He let me know that someone could have come in and done bodily harm to me. I thanked him for his concern... whew!

Our date of departure is drawing nearer. I sure hope that we will be able to get to Kumasi... Ghana's cultural center.

Tuesday, August 18 - Up early again. I have been doing back exercises daily and neck exercises most days. Today I get both exercises done. The breakfast today was heavy. I will be totally surprised if I have not put on a few pounds. Rex has not yet gone back to work. It must be great to be the boss. She is guiding Amarkai to tailor shops where he can get some dresses made to take home. At one of the shops, I buy a bubu and head piece for my mother and Aunt Dot.

At another place, we were able to get more 'Welcome to Ghana' posters. Time seems to be rapidly winding down. Everything that we are going to do has to be done this week. I wrote some more post cards. Of some addresses, I am uncertain. Temporarily I have an extra post card. Then Amarkai asks me for it. He said he was going to write Goldblatt one of his work chums.

His card was mixed with mine. While a passenger in the car, I was leafing through the cards thinking they were all mine. I began reading his card to Goldblatt. He made references (light I hope) to being in Ghana with the Africans in the trees. Granted, it was not my business, but nonetheless I felt that it was incumbent upon me to let him know the tone of his card was disappointing.

That touched a sore spot. We argued back and forth... forth and back. When we got to Sam's office, he and Sister Nana (who was in the car with us) went in. I stayed outside and talked with Abi who will soon move to the states. His wife is already there. I went to the bathroom which is used by several offices in the building. Each office has a key. When I came out, Sam, Amarkai, and Sister Nana were ready to leave.

Amarkai had to use the bathroom, so I gave him the key. He asked me to walk down that way, because he had something to tell me. Obviously irritated at our earlier quid pro quo, he told me that I lacked wisdom because I didn't wait until we were alone to confront him. That certainly makes sense, but the discovery was such that my response was immediate. He added that his comment had been facetious.

When told that he had hit me with some zingers irrespective of who was around. As an example, I disliked his Obruni reference to me. Obruni most often refers to whites, but it may be used for others not from Ghana. I resented it. His response was that when I told him about it, he stopped. I told him that now I will stop. Amarkai added that he and Goldblatt have a unique relationship where he can tease Goldblatt about the Arabs having been in Israel prior to the Jews.

By that I was somewhat taken aback, because I would mention that to any Jew without having to hoist Africans to an imaginary tree. What I found humorous is that he first said he would not send the card, but now he had decided to send it. My response was so be it... that decision is yours. From that point on, the tension between us was high. To me, Amarkai said little and less. To Amarkai, I said little and less.

Together we went to Kofi's shop to pick up some clothing articles. They were not ready. Kofi has a unique high pitched voice (not unlike some designers seen in the movies). He says things like... "Ooh Mrs. E-Kooban". In any event, the clothes are to be ready tomorrow.

Other purchases were made at the Arts Center. I was charged for something I did not get. Hopefully, it can be straightened out tomorrow. At the Art Center, we bumped into the U. S. people (Kim Singleton And Carol Jones) who we met in Elmina. They had planned to go to Kumasi, but have since decided against going. Tentatively we are trying to get to Kumasi on Thursday. Tomorrow I should find out whether I will be leaving for the U. S. on Friday or Monday.

When we get home, we have dinner which is rice, banku, and okra soup. For dessert, there is pineapple, coconut, and sugar cane. One helping is not enough. Rex pleads/cajoles me to take more. Hopefully, I won't burst. After dinner, Rex and I sit down and talk about Ghana and the states.

To me, Rex explains that in Ghana many families have help around the house. Sometimes the help is paid money, and at other times, money may be put into an account for them. If they have not been receiving pay, when they leave, it is expected that they will receive something, e.g. sewing machine, money, or something else of value. Her current maid/house girl (Akos) has been with her for five years.

Rex touched on the extended family concept that seems so prevalent in Ghana. It is not uncommon for a 'family' to be comprised of the parent's children, children of relatives or friends, et al. Rex also mentioned that my behavior was not ever 'demanding' as so many from America who she had met. The others seemed to elevate themselves above Africans. While we were talking, the news came on the tellie, and Rex wanted to watch it. After awhile, I excused myself and went back to my room.

Joy is the first to come back, then Ursula, and believe it or not Jojo. I was so surprised at seeing Jojo that I did not notice Adolph when he came in. All of them, except Ursula, are interviewed on video. Ursula absolutely refuses. She says tomorrow, but I respond that tomorrow never comes, because tomorrow is today. The comment brings a warm smile to Ursula's face.

For a few days, Ursula has been saying that Joy is a naughty boy without ever explaining why. Today she decides to write the reason on her hand. I look for my glasses to better read what is written. Ursula forbids me to put on my glasses. Even without glasses, I can see "S - E - X". Joy giggles.

Joy says that he has to get ready for school but repeatedly leaves and re-enters the room. Finally Joy again asks me to pray for him. Once again, Jojo responds "Joy is sick".

Does a 16 year old boy who dreams about sex warrant prayer to rectify that. I think not, but what is your opinion? When Amarkai comes in the room, he doesn't say anything and neither do I. It seems a bit silly but so be it.

AKOSOMBO DAM

Wednesday, August 19 - I get my exercises out of the way, and then I shower. Amarkai announces today's itinerary, i.e. a visit to the Akosombo Dam. It is the world's largest manmade lake (Volta). It is thought to be approximately 250 miles long. At its conception, it was referred to as the Volta River Project by Osagyefo (Kwame Nkrumah) The project involved the exploitation of the country's bauxite-aluminum resources by means of a huge dam and hydro-electric power station.

When we get to Sam's office, he is not there, but he left instructions for us to wait for him. Before getting into Sam's office, a young 'brother' approached me. He wanted my address, since he hoped to get to the states for the World Cup/1996 Olympics. Additionally, he gave me his address and a free newspaper... The Independent.

Later Amarkai told me that the young 'brother' may write requesting sneakers, money, a ticket, or something of that nature. Some of the youth are so fed up with their plight that they try anything to escape. There was alleged to be a grossly overweight and unattractive African from America working in the Peace Corps. One of the Ghanaian brothers pursued her, and they eventually married. When they got to the states, he cut her loose, i.e. went his own way.

I stopped at the Arts Center, where I thought I was charged for an item that I did not buy. It seems the receipt was inaccurate. Where two items were written, it should have only been one.

Amarkai and I ironed out our differences. I bruised his eye (smile), and he surrendered. Seriously, we talked it out. Everything seems to be o.k. On our way to the dam, we pass the Shai Hills and the

Atumpoko bridge. While in the area, we go into the Volta Hotel, and restaurant, which is very nice. To me, the rates are similar to many hotel rates in America.

Shai Hills

Part of Adome Bridge
(one of Ghana's largest
suspension bridges)

There is beautiful shrubbery surrounding the hotel. Outside the hotel, we find a rock that was found during the dewatering of the Volta River. A ring around a hole in the rock is thought to infer animal fertility. In Ghana, rock engravings are rare. It is believed that the rock is more than 2000 years old. In the area, we see mountains, mango trees, residences of those who worked on the dam and chalets where the more affluent live. As we maneuver around, we get a good view of the Akosombo dam with its turbines, an exit for the overflow, and a back view of the dam. The ferry is docked, and we enter a bar like area on the ferry.

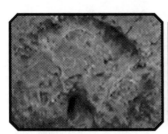

Rock (more than
2000 years old)

Akosombo Dam with
closed spillways

Outlet for excess water

View from Volta Hotel

Volta Hotel rates

Amarkai and Sam
(Volta Hotel balcony)

Will and Sam entering ferry

Fresh water lakes
for fish farms

Presidential (J, J, Rawlimngs
at that time) retreat

Amarkai gets in a friendly debate with a group socializing there. I think they were debating whether the route of the ferry was north or not. There was a lot of laughter, and someone asked Amarkai if he was a teacher. Amidst the laughter, Amarkai confessed that he was once a teacher.

As we were leaving the ferry, we sighted a hospital ship. The name of the ship was Onipanua which in Akan translates 'my fellow human being'. Collectively, for humanitarian reasons, we all hoped that the hospital ship was not used often.

Prevalent in the area were fresh water lakes where fish farming was done with fresh water fish such as whiting and talapia. On a hill, there was a house that was used as a presidential retreat. The area is highly fortified, and entry can only be gained through the air or one road. It is used in much the same way as the Peduase Lodge. The trip to Akosombo was nice. We took a lot of video in that area.

Sunday we are scheduled to take a ferry ride around the lake, but it is uncertain. The security officer told us if we planned to come, we should be there by 9:30 a.,m. He said the area will be filled with cars especially those belonging to 'Obruni'. When questioned, he further explained that his Obruni reference was to whites. The name of the ferry is 'Dodi Princess'.

DUBOIS CULTURAL CENTER

Although not yet confirmed, it seems that my U. S. return will be Sunday. Tomorrow I may know for certain. The latest in house rumor has us leaving early Friday morning for Kumasi and returning that night. That same day, Friday, the Kumasi Festival begins.

After dinner, I laid down across the bed. The time was about 8 p.m. I did not awaken until the following morning at 5:50 a.m.

Thursday, August 20 - When I awakened, I heard noises outside my window. Through the curtain, I could see Izzi, the gardener, tending to the plants next to the protective wall. How are you I asked Izzi. He smiled and nodded affirmatively. Akos, the house girl, walked by singing a song in one of the Ghanain languages. She seemed to be quite happy.

I went to the living room to see if any of the young men were around. I needed some toilet paper. As I got closer, I could hear that 'church' was in session. Quietly I turned around and returned to my room. In a few minutes, Joy came to my room. I asked him to get me some toilet paper, and he complied. When he returned, he played the gospel song that he had played once before. Sung in the Twi language, this time Joy says that the song has something to do with God being King.

His thoughts turn to what am I going to leave him when I depart. With a straight face, I tell him that I will leave my warm hand shake and ask him if that is enough. His reply is no. I countered with 'he who is not thankful for a little is not worthy of a lot'. Joy said he agreed with that. Without a doubt, I am certain that I will think of something to leave with Joy.

We drive down to the office, but Sam is not there. It seems that he left a few minutes before we arrived and went to check on my return ticket. Instead of just waiting, I suggested that we visit the W. E. B. DuBois Cultural Center. One of the office messengers gave us directions that would put us in the area of the center. In that vicinity, Amarkai asked a motorcycle policeman where was the center located. The center is in the Cantoments area which is a very affluent district. At one time, the U. S. Embassy was located in that area.

The policeman and Amarkai spoke in Twi. Since the policeman was going that way, he suggested that we follow him. I thought about my last encounter with a policeman in America. It was far from cordial. At the center, there were displays outside and inside. To enter, the charge was 600 cedis. DuBois had been commissioned by Kwame Nkrumah to write the Encyclopedia Africana. At Dubois' death, he was a Ghanaian citizen. W. E. B. DuBois had been integral in the struggle for black equality in America.

Bust of DuBois outside cultural center

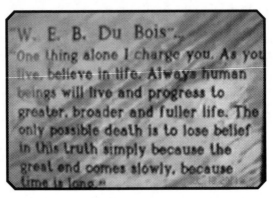

"W. E. B. Du Bois".
One thing alone I charge you. As you live, believe in life. Always human beings will live and progress to greater, broader and fuller life. The only possible death is to lose belief in this truth simply because the great end comes slowly, because time is long."

DuBois passage

Picture taking was allowed outside but not inside. Inside the building, there were photos of African notables. To name a few, there was Cheik Anta Diop (the Senegalese physicist and historian), Marcus Garvey, Paul Robeson, Kwame Nkrumah, Shaka Zulu, et al. There was a video on DuBois' death; As we sat and watched, Amarkai tried to take a few video shots. I am certain that he was seen by the tour guide, but she pretended not to see him taking video.

Stevie Wonder, the entertainer, had visited the center last month. Inside there were photos of him laying a wreath. From there, we went to pick up the girls from school and take them home. Oh! Today another family member showed up. She has been away at the university. Not unlike Joy, she has that British talk down pat.

We again went to the tailor shop to see if Amarkai's order was ready. Once again, it was not. From there, we went to the Arts Center. Mrs. Ekluban negotiated all my purchases there. She bargains very well. I think she was particularly impressed at the price (4000 cedis) she bargained for a dress to enhance her own wardrobe. While Rex was bargaining for some gifts Amarkai wanted to take home, Amarkai left us and went to another area to bargain some items for his son.

Will looking - Rex bargaining pleasantly

On the way home, we stopped at an area, Chemunaa, where Amarkai's sister and brother (Amerley and Victor) would be. Both his siblings are older than he is, but his sister looks younger. He feebly tried not to agree with me.

When we get home, there is fufu for dinner. What has long since become the norm, Rex, once again, piles and piles food on my plate. I, who was about 155 pounds, now feel at least 200 pounds.

On television, there is a show about the Ashanti people. Much of it revolves around the aura of the Asantehene. When a dignitary comes to shake his hand, an aid must move his hand to where the dignitary has his hand waiting... whew.

Tomorrow at 5 a.m., we are scheduled to leave for Kumasi (the Garden City) an Ashanti stronghold. Oh! At the DuBois Museum, earlier today, were two African American women. One was from Detroit and the other from Baltimore. They seemed not to realize that I was from the U. S. One of them, helping us understand

DuBois, felt compelled to tell us that Harvard, one of the schools DuBois attended, was one of America's top schools. Additionally, she made us aware of how difficult things were for blacks during the DuBois era.

Amarkai asked if DuBois' wife was white. The woman exclaimed "Oh no! Her skin was like mine". I told the lady... oh... she was paper sack brown. While the woman was smiling, I told her that I too was from the USA.

KUMASI FESTIVAL

I am going to bed. Tomorrow morning, I have to wake up early for Kumasi. Time is really short. There are only three more days in Ghana. Good night!

Friday, August 21 - It seems that all of us are up early this morning. We were ready to depart about 5:15 a.m. Although he was up, Sam was not ready to leave when we were. It must have been close to 6 a.m. when we actually left. Kukua, who I met yesterday, is going back to school. She will accompany us. Her school, University of Science and Technology is in Kumasi which is today's destination.

Since we left for Kumasi, before breakfast, we stop to get something to eat. I had sardines inside a bread patty and pineapple juice. As to what the others bought, I am uncertain, but Kukua bought some bread that we shared in route. Nica, who also came with us, brought water.

The trip takes close to four hours. When we arrive at the cultural grounds, activity seems to be slight. There isn't much going on. A parade has started toward town, and it will end up back here at the grounds. Some people are setting up their booths for the festival. Others are already set up. Musicians are warming up.

Parading into town

A tribe arriving to the festival

Drummers warming up for the festival

Drying cassava which will later be pounded for fufu at restaurant

Sam and Will debating how close Will has come to 'flavoring' Sam

Another African child (Kukua) - Amarkai's prideful designation

Pounding fufu (other meals thought heresy)
for patrons at the restaurant

Amarkai looks at an Oware game. Sam buys the game rule book for him. I purchase a cane that Kathy had asked me to purchase for her husband. Since things are still a bit slow, we choose to go to lunch. Perhaps after lunch, more will be happening. The restaurant is a rough (physically) looking spot, but Sam says it has a reputation for making great fufu. If truth is told, I didn't want fufu, but Sam says it is heresy to order any food but fufu in Kumasi.

While waiting, we take some pictures. It must be 35 to 40 minutes that we have been waiting. The restaurant was not open when we arrived. There is an ever increasing line of people waiting to get served. Finally we are served. Amarkai cleaned his bowl. All the others, except me, left a little in their bowls. I left a lot. For some reason that fufu agreed less with me.

On leaving, I had to go to the bathroom... to urinate. There was an open area where one could step in and take care of business. I am elated that I did not have to defecate. As I mentioned earlier, men urinating publicly is a common occurrence. In route to Kumasi, all the men had to go. Sam pulled the car over, and we went. Just knowing the women were there made me uncomfortable, but when you have to go... you have to go.

Back at the park, spectators were setting up chairs for themselves. We did the same for ourselves. Kukua carried my video bag and got my chair... you know the little things that a young woman should do. Amarkai had been told that he needed a permit to take video. There were a host of people taking videos including Obruni. Consequently, Amarkai chose to film until someone stopped him. No one ever did. He resembled a member of the press as he mingled with them on and off the field.

Entertaining the crowd   Unknown tribe dancing

Performing at festival

The Dagombo tribe from North Ghana

Dagombo tribe

Talking drums 'speak'
and are understood

The dancers were great especially the Dagombo tribe from the northern part of Ghana. My problem was they did not dance long enough. Tribes from throughout Ghana performed at the festival. Some danced. Many came onto the field with their chiefs or queen mothers. The pageantry was spectacular. Finally Otumfuo Opokuware made his entrance. He is the king of all the Ashanti tribes. One of his subjects held an umbrella for him. Upon his entrance, everyone seated must stand. When he sits, everyone else may take their seats.

At the moment, he is prepared to speak, another subject brings a microphone to him. To stand, on his own, is thought too much for Otumfuo. Consequently, he sits and speaks. He speaks to the throngs in the Twi language. He claims not to know English. In the Twi language, Otumfuo translates to 'Almighty'.

When the Otumfuo is selected, he is said to be 'in-stooled' probably because of the significance of the Golden Stool in Ashanti folklore.

Otumfuo Opokuware carried onto the
festival grounds by his subjects

When the Otumfuo walks to the stands, protocol dictates that everyone stand and remain standing until he sits.

KUMASI FESTIVAL

(THE GOLDEN STOOL)

*Y*ears *ago in the West African village of Awukugwa (A - woo koo gua), there was a husband and wife (Egya Ano: Ehja Ahno and Mame Ekubea: Eh koo beh) who had been unable to have children. Among their people, marriage was not thought to be binding until a child was born.*

*The villagers called barren women **OBONIN** and childless men **OKRAWA**. Because of their childless relationship, they went to the Fetish Priest and asked for help. After a period of time, a child, Kwame Frimpong, was born to the couple.*

The birth was somewhat odd, because the baby was born with a fetish stick in his hand. When the mother put the baby to bed, upon looking in on the baby later, Kwame Frimpong would have vanished. This event repeated itself so often that three days after the last disappearance, the parents returned to the Fetish Priest to seek advice.

*The Fetish told the parents that feeding Kwame impaterea (em pah treh), the stream fish, and goat was causing the problem. He cautioned Egya Ano and Mame Ekubea to **ALWAYS** keep Kwame Frimpong on a diet that allowed him to **NEVER** eat the impaterea fish or the goat meat. The parents were very thankful and promised to follow the advice of the Fetish Priest.*

While growing up, Kwame Frimpong began to perform wondrous acts. On seeing these wonders, the villagers would exclaim Anoykye. Anoykye means look. One time, he picked up some wood from the ground and made an Oware game with his bare hands. In unison, the villagers exclaimed ANOYKYE.

The word, anoykye, was used so often when referring to one of Kwame Frimpong's wondrous feats that the villagers began to call him Anoykye. Because he was different, many of the elders hated Anoykye. Their jealousy prompted some of them to tell the village chief, Ansah SesereEku (seh seh reh koo) that Anoykye was dangerous and plotting to kill the chief. The chief believed what he was told and had Anoykye imprisoned.

Some time later, Osei Tutu, a member of one of the ASHANTI royal families, visited the prison. On one of his visits, he met Anoykye. Osei Tutu seemed impressed with Anoykye. Anoykye told Osei Tutu that one day he (Osei) would become a very strong and powerful chief. The two became very good friends.

Soon Osei became a chief of one of the ASHANTI villages. He liked and was so impressed with the prisoner, Anoykye, that Chief Osei Tutu went to Anoykye's village chief and asked that he have Anoykye released from prison. Anoykye was then released from prison.

*Chief Osei Tutu asked his friend, Anoykye, to come and live in his village of **KWAMAN**. Because his own villagers disliked him so much, Anoykye agreed to live in the village of **KWAMAN**.*

*On a Friday morning, Anoykye asked Chief Osei Tutu to call all the ASHANTI chiefs together for a meeting. The wondrous Anoykye told the chiefs that he would summon a **GOLDEN STOOL** from the heavens adding that the stool would make the ASHANTI strong and bind them together as one nation. Anoykye told the chiefs that they needed a meeting place where they could meet and plan strategies. He planted tree seeds in the villages of **KUMAWU, KWAMAN** and **DWABEN**. The village where the seed would grow would be declared the headquarters.*

*The seed grew in **KWAMAN** where Osei was chief. The ASHANTI kingdoms became one nation, and Osei Tutu became the **CHIEF OF***

*CHIEFS (Asantehene). The golden stool was referred to as **SIKA GUA KOFI**. Sika meaning gold and gua Kofi because the stool was summoned on a Friday. Soon Anoykye would be called Okomfo Anoykye ... the great priest who does wonders.*

*During his life-time, Okomfo Anoykye never had time for women, but he did meet a woman to whom he became very attached. They began to see each other on a regular basis and were married in **ASHANTI**. One day, his wife fed Okomfo the impaterea fish that the Fetish Priest said he should never eat. A bone from the fish stuck in Okomfo's throat.*

Okomfo announced that he was going to his room to cure himself and would remain there for one week. All were instructed to wait one week but not to cry should he not come out in one week.

One week passed, and there was great concern because Okomfo had not come out. A strong odor came from the room, and everyone thought that Okomfo Anoykye had surely died. The people began to cry.

*When they entered the room, they found Okomfo Anoykye dead. According to the legend had they not cried, Okomfo would have lived. Okomfo Anoykye died in **CHIAPATEREE (chia-pa tre)**..*

The golden stool at the Kumasi Festival

It is said that replicas of the golden stool are often on display, but for important Ashanti functions, the true stool is displayed. In the photo, one of the Asantehene's men seems to tire in the heat from the weight of the stool. He seems to be wiping his face with a handkerchief while getting assistance from a fellow tribesman.

The Ashanti are primarily a matrilineal tribe and fall under the Akan umbrella along with the Akuapim, Akyem, Fanti, and Kwahu. Ashanti speak the Twi language.

Statue of Okomfo Anoykye summoning the golden stool
(Kumasi, Ghana)

Tribe at festival

Chief and tribe welcoming Will

Another Chief and tribe welcoming Will

Queen Mother and her tribe welcoming Will back home

It is close to 4 p.m., and we have to make the trek back to Accra. Lest I forget, on our way to Kumasi, Sam bought plantain and snail and left them in the bed of the truck. Both Amarkai and I asked if that was a good move. We wondered if a possible theft was made easier. Kukua and Sam are convincing as they explain that Kumasi is a farming area where food is plentiful. They insisted that no one would bother the food. As we prepare to leave, they are proven to be correct. The food has not been touched. Can you imagine that happening anywhere in the USA.

Amarkai stopped to buy some brandy for his grandfather, the old man, who sang the tribal song with Amarkai and me our first week in Ghana. Then it was hello. Tonight it will be so long... until next time.

At the university where we dropped Kukua, Mensa a former student of Amarkai's came to see us and said hello. If I have not mentioned it, prior to coming to the states, Amarkai was a teacher. His version is that he was a master teacher... hmm. While we were there, Oswald, Amarkai's brother, also came down to see us.

When we get home, it is close to 9 p.m. Dinner is ready, and we eat. Quite expectedly, Rex piles on food for me. It is time for a shower, and I am eager to comply and go to bed. Tonight seems so strange, since only two more nights remain on my first trip to Ghana... West Africa.

D - DAY MINUS 1

Saturday, August 22 - Last night, I was in bed about 12 midnight. This morning, I am up at 6:30a.m. We had church this morning. A-Men. Nana Sam gave the benedicfion. During service, it appeared that Amarkai fell asleep. Back in my room, I heard a soft tap on the door. It was Nica. She gathered up the dirty clothes. Since tomorrow is Sunday, it seems quite likely that today's wash will be our last one. IT WAS GREAT WHILE IT LASTED!

Joy came by my room. He wanted that religious tape. Today he is cleaning the cars. My suspicions are that he will clean to the beat of the religious tape. I must be right. Through the windows, I can hear the music.

Amarkai looked at some land that he is considering purchasing. From there we head to the Art Center to get permits that will allow us to carry non antiques, e.g. xylophone, chief's stool, outside the country. On the way to the phone center, I had to urinate badly. I went to the back and took care of business. Sam told me that it was a good thing that I was not caught. Where I went was an illegal urinating spot. There is a nice bathroom inside.

We drove to all the places where we had clothing orders to complete and picked up those items. When we went home to eat, Rex piled it on again. Rex reflected "in a few more days, you won't have to worry about this harassment". She thinks that if I don't eat somehow she is being inhospitable. Nothing can be farther from the truth. Sam and Rex have been hosts extraordinaire... the nonpareil. The fact remains... I am not a big eater.

Video from Kumasi was played. I think there was some excellent footage. Additionally, we viewed the video from my visit to Nana Sam's church (Gethsemene Methodist Church).

Nica came to my room to pack our bags. She was so dedicated to the task at hand, she mixed some of my things with Amarkai's. He and I will have to straighten that out later.

Sunday, August 23 - Today is D - Day our day of departure which in many ways is also a depressing day. For me, it is truthfully painful. I am still moving things around with respect to packing.

Reflecting a bit, I would not have been privy to this experience had I not come with Amarkai and lived in a private home. There certainly are some cultural differences. Although many of the Ghanaians have accepted Christianity, they seem to have blended in some of their own traditions such as the dance associated with the 'day of the week' offering.

The 'bribe' concept I detest, but the extended family seems to be a positive. To repeat, here the children of brothers are considered brothers and sisters... not cousins. In a like manner the children of sisters are considered brothers and sisters.

Amarkai is going to church with Rex, and I am going with Sam. Sam and Rex seem to be competing to see with which one Amarkai will go to church. Again, Amarkai decides to wear kente draped over his shoulder and challenges me to do the same.

I felt uncomfortable trying to hold it on. Additionally, I remember Kukua talking about some people who don't drape it over correctly. That thought was enough for me... out of the kente into a suit.

We were running late (Amarkai's fault), so we detoured to another church. It was Pentecostal. They get down... rhythm nation. I was given the VIP treatment and introduced to the church. All visitors are greeted with a unique rhythmic ten count clap. They also do 'the dance'. I had only one camcorder battery today, and it died as the whole church seemed to begin talking in tongue.

During the minister's sermon, one woman fell at his feet. To me, it seemed that she attempted to grab his legs, but he nimbly stepped aside as she hit the floor. On the floor, she lay crying and shaking. The minister went on with his sermon while another woman put a blanket over the woman on the floor. After a few moments, the woman on the floor got up and sat down.

When we got home, Rex told me that Amarkai had trouble with his kente. It seems that he has forgotten how to wear it. Is this the same person who tried to coerce me into wearing kente? I didn't have to say a word. Mrs. Ekuban had said enough. The Brit, a former Ghanain, Amarkai, had failed miserably at attempting to blush.

Time to get to the airport is drawing nearer. The three and one half weeks have truly flown by. Everyone stops by the room to say good-bye. Rex even sends another dish of plantain. Fulash likes one of my caps, and I tell him it is his. I think Joy wanted it, but they all get something. Amarkai and I pool our remaining cedis and split them equally among the children.

Good-bye is particularly tough. Our bags are put into the truck, and we head for Kotoka International Airport. Some are in the truck, and the overflow (Rex, et al) are in the car. At the airport, we don't have to pay for the extra pieces of luggage, i.e. stool and xylophone. The baggage people tell me that the xylophone has to be crated, but the stool does not.

The Brit (Amarkai) attempting kente

While Amarkai and I are worried about our $200 deposit for the camcorders, there is a white guy, claiming to be a citizen of Ghana, who is at least equally worried. The customs person says that the money is in the bank. We all look at each other. Amarkai and the other guy continue to talk to the customs agent who finally goes to the safe to get the money. The white guy and Amarkai give him a few cedis.

I give him nothing, and he seems to expect nothing. My thoughts tell me that they may have jumped the gun concerning the bribe. Glee is only short lived. Amarkai tells me that he included me in his payment... sorry.

In the terminal, sweat is dropping profusely from my face. It is hot. As hot as it has been while in Ghana, not one time have I heard a person ask... what is the temperature. Melody buys me A handkerchief to wipe the sweat from my face. That was very nice of her, and I let her know it. Of course, Amarkai has to editorialize when he tells me that Ghanaians seldom use tissues... hence the use of handkerchiefs. We warmly embrace all our hosts and say our final good-byes as Amarkai and I head for the plane. It was truly touching.

Our flight is from Accra to Abidjan to Gatwick in London. There was one observation that I found interesting. When the plane left Accra and again in Abidjan, personnel went from the cockpit to the tail of the plane... decontaminating the plane with some kind of spray. Leaving London for Accra, I saw no such action. Other passengers on the plane seemed to agree that such was a routine occurrence when leaving Accra. One man mentioned that he had experienced the fumigation when leaving Lagos, Nigeria.

There's one perception I cannot avoid
It... on or off... I cannot flick
I'm black with symptoms of the paranoid
However... I may not be 'sick'

I find the flight not very eventful, although I lost my glasses on the plane. The Brit (Mr. Big Stuff) berated me for that. I allowed Mr. Big Stuff to assume responsibility for the cane bought for Kathy's husband and a few other smaller items. The cane displayed the theme... see no evil; hear no evil; speak no evil. We rode the Speedlink from Gatwick to Heathrow.

From the Speedlink window, Amarkai saw his uncle waiting for our arrival. The little fellow (little Freddie) was so elated that he left the cane and some other items on the bus. When I noticed his carelessness, it was too late. The bus had moved on. Of course, it was incumbent upon me to berate him for his lack of responsibility... whew!

It was from Amarkai's uncle that we learned of the devastation Hurricane Andrew had on southern Florida.

Having to leave Ghana has made me more than a little down. It seems that everything else is anti climatic. What Ghanaians say, I believe is true...

Ghanaians made me welcome and confident
though I was late returning home
It was my first trip to the continent
My return... had taken too long

THE JIGSAW PUZZLE

When I went to pick up my luggage at Newark International Airport, I received some bad news. My crated package, the NgE Nyame chief's stool, in flight, had been broken into a number of splintered pieces... resembling a jigsaw puzzle. Someone speculated that customs people may have been searching for drugs. There was no attempt to mask my disappointment.

I notified the airlines immediately and was apprised of the course of action necessary for compensation. For a period of time, the bench remains were just at home taking up space. After some time had elapsed, I told my son that I was going to throw the remnants in the trash.

He asked me not to, adding that he could possibly do something with it. I agreed not to trash it but wondered what could possibly be done. For another period of time, the stool fragments again took up space.

One night, I returned home entering through the garage. As I walked through the house door, in the middle of the floor was a rebuilt chief's stool. To me, it was remarkably done and must have taken lots of time and patience. One would have to examine the stool more than thoroughly to detect that the pieces had been perfectly put and glued together a la a jigsaw puzzle. I was truly taken aback and remembered that I had favored trashing the uneven fragments.

My son was in bed asleep, so I didn't say anything to him that night. The following morning, I thanked him again and again. I have shared the story often.

SCIENCE V MOM

Born 'Willie' … with a surname that is moot
In school … I was nicknamed 'The Shoe'
The Fanti … put me closer to my root
Now for my name … I know 'Kweku'

Fascinated by the Fanti names associated with the day of the week in which one is born, I was eager to discover my day of the week. On my return to work, I got on the PC, went to a calendar site, and input the month, day, and year in which I was born. Quickly, I learned that I was born on a Wednesday. That instant Will became Kweku. I still answer to Will, but I feel more strongly linked to Kweku.

To share that information with my mother, I called her immediately. Thinking that I had something on her, I asked… *on what day of the week was I born*. To my surprise, she answered rapidly that I was born on Wednesday and was quick to add days of the week for my four brothers and my son who was born on Tuesday. Unable to contain myself, I released a loud laugh.

Of course, my mother wanted to know why I was laughing. I told her that I had wasted time going to the world of science to get the information when I could have just called her. Born on Tuesday, my son liked the name Kwabina.

I wish that I could truly share with you the joy I received from my trip to Ghana. For me, it was very important. I was both touched and moved. In no way, can I recommend that everybody go, since everybody probably would not enjoy the trip as I did. For those who choose to go, I will suggest that they leave some of that 'American privilege' ego at home. Learn and show willingness to adapt. The conditions at the home where I lived were comfortable. Every place I visited was not state of the art. All the people I visited were not people of means. Each toilet call was not at a convenient place. Many Ghanaians have had negative experiences with some people from the U. S.

BACK AT WORK

For those of African descent who run from anything 'African'. Whether you like it or not... admit to it or not... you still have an African root from somewhere on that continent. People have begun to ask me... are you going back. My answer is most definitely... the first chance I get. Although I have seen so little, I know that I love 'Mother Africa'. I would love to help improve the good and eliminate the bad. Before leaving this earth, I want to see as much as I can of the African continent.

There was a Nigerian fellow at work who always spoke but never lingered in my company. At lunch and other breaks, he was always with a white woman. I don't know that anyone knew, but most assumed that they were dating. On my first day back to work, he approached me and mentioned that he heard that I had visited Ghana.

The lunch period had ended, but we continued to talk about my experience. His female friend seemed to have grown tired of waiting for him and asked him to go with her. Politely, he told her to go ahead, and he would catch up with her later. We continued to talk. Somehow there must be something significant to that whole dynamic.

My effervescence at my visit prompted an African American woman, who had been to the continent, to conclude that with me, my exuberance over Ghana was just a fad. Surely there must be a 'teaching moment' there someplace.

Another old friend, who had also visited West Africa, opined at how terrible the African people lived. Some Caucasians 'allowed' me to say what I wanted about the trip. Others wanted to know about the safari which still seemed their default motive for going to any part of Africa.

THE BLISSFULLY IGNORANT

An African American 'complimented' Amarkai's niece (born in Ghana) at how quickly she had learned to wear clothes. I enjoyed the niece's response. "Thank you... these clothes are so much more comfortable than my fig leaf was". An East African student, at one of the large universities, was asked by his white roommate if he knew how to sleep on a pillow.

A female student in America had made plans to go back to her African country for the summer. She was catching a bus to Philadelphia. A few of her white classmates wanted to know if that was where she would begin walking home to Kenya. She nodded affirmatively. Expressing their concern, those classmates asked if she would be back in time for the next semester. She again assured them that she would. Then concern shifted to the condition of her tree where she lived. "It must be bushy" they opined. The Kenyan girl assured them that someone was trimming the bushes in 'her' tree, and it would be fine.

Contemplating a church visit, the African minister was asked where would the plane land. The minister very skillfully comforted the potential visitors when he let them know that he would have some of the church's young people clear landing space for the plane.

When I returned to playing pinochle with my old buddies, some, one more than the others, found it impossible to say Kweku (Quay-koo). The names I was called were not decipherable in any language. There was a lot of jest involved, but when I asked the name of the former governor of California... *Schwarzenegger* was quickly enunciated quite clearly. I chuckled before he understood what had happened. Then we all chuckled.

I don't know that my visit to Ghana has enlightened anyone other than myself which incidentally is what the trip was purported to do. Rome wasn't built in a day and neither was Accra.

At that time (1992), for too many, in my view, Africa remained the 'dark continent'. Perhaps on that, there was a quasi agreement between some blacks and whites. To slightly augment an Akan proverb, *we cannot tell the good from the bad because of pretense, hypocrisy, and sometimes ignorance.*

A BRIEF POLITICAL HISTORY OF GHANA

Present day Ghana was formerly known as the Gold Coast. The Portuguese were one of the first European countries to come to that area in the late 15th century. They built forts, castles, etc. that were used as trading posts with the Gold Coast. Ivory and gold were the main exports of the Portuguese. That trade was replaced by the slave trade.

In 1897, British troops occupied the Gold Coast. The Gold Coast was annexed by the British in 1901. British direct rule replaced traditional authority in the Gold Coast. Responding to a grievance from Gold Coast servicemen police fired their weapons at them in the 1940's.

In August 1947, nationalists of Gold Coast founded the United Gold Coast Convention and asked Kwame Nkrumah to lead their campaign for self government. A riot took place when Nkrumah and others were jailed after troops fired on demonstrators.

Kwame Nkrumah attended, Lincoln University, an American historically black university in Pennsylvania. Some say he was influenced by the book 'Philosophy and Opinions' by Marcus Garvey. In 1948, he was jailed and detained by the British. To get more citizens involved in the political process, Nkrumah formed the Convention Peoples Party (CPP) in 1949.

After being imprisoned and tried in 1951, Kwame Nkrumah was released and asked by the British to form a government. By this time, he had become a major figure in the fight for Ghana independence. Fellow citizens fondly referred to Nkrumah as Osagyefu whose Fanti translation to English is freedom fighter.

From 6 March 1957 to 1960, he headed Ghana's transitional government. On 1 July 1960, Nkrumah became the head of state for Ghana's first republic. In 1966, Nkrumah traveled to Hanoi for a Non Aligned Nations meeting. His absence from Ghana proved to be an opportune moment for the 1966 Senior Officers Coup D'état. That coup is now thought to have had CIA involvement.

The coup was led by Major General J. A. Ankrah and Colonel Emanuel Kwasi Kotoka. They joined with Major A. A. Afrifa to form the National Liberation Council (NLC).

An aborted coup was led by Air Force captains Hadley and Arthur. The then Lt. General Kotoka was killed in the airport area that now bears his name. Lt. General Ankrah replaced Kotoka in the government. For taking bribes, Ankrah was replaced by Afrifa. Afrifa arranged the transition to the second republic which lasted from 1969 to 1972.

Dr. K. A. Busia became the head of state for the second republic forming the Progress party. In 1972, the senior officers pulled a coup d'état and formed the National Redemption Council (NRC) which evolved into the Supreme Military Council led by Colonels I. K. Acheampong, F. W. K. Akuffo and Odartey-Wellington. All of whom became generals.

During a palace coup, on 4 June 1979, Akuffo replaced Acheampong. It was called the Junior Officer's Coup. The Armed Forces Revolutionary Council was led by Flight Lieutenant J. J. Rawlings who was arrested and put under court martial proceedings. During the process, Rawlings is said to have demanded "Leave my men alone... I alone am responsible for everything".

When Rawlings was arrested, Afrifa wrote a letter to Akuffo. In the letter, he wrote if Rawlings is not removed from the system, one day Rawlings will line all of them up and kill them. The letter was printed in a Ghana daily newspaper While Rawlings was in jail, A few junior officers led by Captains Kwashikah and Pattington along with Sergeant Alolga Akatapori engineered an uprising that freed Rawlings to lead their uprising.

All the senior officers, except General Odartey-Wellington, attempted to flee. Wellington killed the men Rawlings had controlling the broadcast media. When he took control, Wellington broadcast that all Ghana air force planes flying should cease flying immediately. Reinforcements of Rawlings' men routed Wellington from the station and chased him to the Nema police station where he was killed. The RECCE (Reconnaissance Corps) Regiment continued to resist until a plea from Rawlings emphasizing that they were not the enemy. When Rawlings took over the government, he announced that there was a need for bloodshed to cleanse the nation. The vetting committee identified participants in all the coups from the 1966 coup until that present time. All those involved were to account for the source of their assets while they were in government.

Afrifa insisted that his wealth was due to an austere life. As an example, he stated that he ate very little. It was deemed a lie. Acheampong, Afrifa, and five other generals were lined up and executed by a firing squad. General Afrifa's words had proven to be prophetic.

General Odartey-Wellington was portrayed as a brave soldier. He was given hero treatment, and at his funeral, there was a 21 gun salute. J. J. Rawlings was one of the pallbearers.

The third republic was from 1979 to 1981. After 3 months, Flight Lieutenant Rawlings returned to the barracks and handed power over to the Peoples National Party (PNP). Dr. Hilla Limann was elected head of state. His number 2 man was Dr. DeGraft Johnson. On 31 December 1981, there was another coup named the December 31st Coup. It was led by J. J. Rawlings who headed the Provincial

(Provisional) National Defense Council (PNDC). An offshoot of the PNDC was the Peoples Defense Council (PDC) which was formed by grass roots politicians. The fourth republic started in early 1993. J. J. Rawlings was elected head of state.

GLOSSARY

Abu tum dam - Words, in a song, that were sung by Amarkai's grandfather, Kweku Bronya Amparbin, to his grandchildren. None of the grandchildren knows what the words mean.

Aburi - A relatively small town northeast of Accra. The town is known for the Botanical Gardens.

Accra - The capital city of Ghana.

Adentsia - Adentsia is an Akan word that means I will see you tomorrow.

Adome Bridge - Ghana's largest suspension bridge. It's on the Volta River near the town of Atimpoku.

Akan - The largest ethnic group in Ghana. Under the Akan umbrella falls the Ashanti, Akuapem, Akyem, Kwahu, Wassa, Fanti, Brong, et al.

Akos - A short form for the Akan name Akosua which is the name for a female born on Sunday.

Akosombo Dam - It is a hydro electric dam on the Volta River in Ghana. The dam was built to provide electricity for the aluminum industry. During its construction, the dam flooded and created Lake Volta the largest (surface area) manmade lake in the world. Many people were displaced and villages were destroyed.

Akyem - One of the tribes ethnically linked to the Akan umbrella. Amarkai's mother was a member of that tribe.

Akwaaba Welcome - A unique welcome that is given to first time visitors or to those who have not been seen in awhile. It begins with a glass of water that is expected to be taken. After the water, a soft drink is brought that the visitor can accept or refuse.

Aprepensa - An Akan meal made from dry roasted corn that has been ground into corn flour.

Asantehene - In 1992 was referred to as Asantehene, Otumfuo Opoko Ware. The Asantehene is the king of the Ashanti people. He ascends to the throne matrilineally.

Atchimota School - Said to be one of the better secondary high schools in Ghana. Attendees are generally from well to do families.

Ayiko/yaaei - In the Akan and Ga languages, ayikoh (ah yee ko) is uttered to congratulate someone for a duty well done. The person acknowledging 'ayiko' responds yaaei (yah yay).

Ayilo - A white clay that fetish priests/priestesses use to cover their bodies. Pregnant women also seek ayilo in a lumpy form. It is thought to be rich in calcium.

Banku - A meal which is a soulful combination of corn, flour, water, and salt. Dry corn is peeled from the cob and mixed with water forming a corn dough (fermented for 3 days). It is then poured into boiling water minus the raw corn.

Botanical Gardens - A tourist attraction north of Accra. The garden is known for its indigenous trees and plants. Dignitaries from around the world often plant trees from other parts of the world.

Bubu - woman's dress

Bukom Market - A busy market in Ghana where food products and other items are sold. Kenkey, banku and smoked fish are big sellers. When dark falls, the market becomes action filled in good and bad ways.

Bush Meat - Meat not raised on a farm. Meat from the grasscutter animal is an example of bush meat.

Cape Coast -The capitol of Ghana before Accra. It is a fishing village known for its secondary schools. Mfantsipim is one of Ghana's best secondary schools as well as being the oldest. Additionally, the University of Cape Coast is there.

Cassava - Cassava is a tuber used to make many Ghanaian food dishes as well as starch.

Cedi - The cedi is Ghana's paper monetary unit. The value with respect to the U. S. dollar varies. Ghana's copper and silver coins are called pesewas.

Christiansborg Castle - Similar to the white house in America. It is also known as the Osu castle. At one time it was used in the slave trade to transport slaves.

Dagomba - A tribe primarily living in northern Ghana

DuBois Cultural Center - A historical museum featuring the works of W. E. B. Dubois who labored for racial equality in the U. S. but died as a citizen of Ghana.

Elmina - A fishing community in Ghana where the Elmiina Castle/ Dungeon was once used in the gold trade. The slave trade replaced the gold trade and captured slaves were held there before they were shipped primarily to Brazil and the Caribbean.

Ewe - One of Ghana's more than 70 tribes. The tribe is patrilineal.

Face the wall - A slang name for kokonte which is thought a poor man's meal. The meal is made from cassava that has gone bad.

Fermented cassava is peeled, cut into pieces, and dried. Soup is poured over the cassava powder and eaten. Kokonte has a dark brown color.

Falasha - An Ethiopian Hebrew group often referred to as the House of Israel or Beta Israel. The religious group is thought to have descended from Menelik (the son of King Solomon and the Queen of Sheba (Makeda)).

Fanti - One of Ghana's tribes falling under the Akan umbrella.

Fetish - Generally followed by priest/priestess who are religious figures in one of the traditional religions.

Frafrah - Is a tribe primarily based in northern Ghana.

Fufu - One of Ghana's staple foods.

Ga - A Ghana tribe found primarily in Accra. Amarkai's father was Ga.

Golden Stool - The ceremonial stool that is said to bind the Ashanti people together. According to legend, it was summoned from the heavens by Okomfu Anoyke.

Gye Nyame - Is an Adrinkra Symbol meaning 'Except God'.

Jollof Rice - A Ghanaian food made from a rice, stew, meat/chicken/fish mixture.

Juju - Magical power that some of the tribal people are believed to have. It is akin to voodoo.

Karkro - A Ghanaian meal made from ripe fermented plantain. Salt, pepper, ginger, and flour are added and pounded into a mixture which is rolled into fist sized balls and fried.

Kenkey - A derivative of banku. When banku is 1/2 cooked, add corn dough (sticky paste) roll fist size from corn husk is a Ga preparation method. The Fanti use plantain or banana leaves instead of the corn husk used by the Ga people.

Kente Cloth - Hand woven (on native loom) fabric native to Ghana. The cloth is multicolored. It is thought to have been first used by the Ashanti people.

Kotoka Airport - Ghana's lone international airport which was named after General Kotoka who was one of the leaders in the coup d'état that overthrew Nkrumah's government. Kotoka was later killed near the airport area during an aborted coup attempt.

Kumasi - An Ashanti stronghold referred to as the Garden City because of its variety in flowers and plants. A countrywide festival is held there annually.

Libation - Pouring libation is a means by which traditional Ghanaians communicate with departed spirits. Alcohol/water is generally used. The procedure takes place when the pourer is thankful for something or requesting help/support in achieving something. The name of the departed is mentioned as the pourer seems to talk with the spirit, and portions of the liquid is poured on the ground intermittently until the liquid is almost empty. The pourer drinks the last portion.

Maaba - An Akan word meaning 'I am back'.

Mama Panyin - In a family Mama Panyin is the elder Mama. An example would be a mother whose mother is living with her. To her children, her mother would be Mama Panyin. The children's mother would be Mama Karaba (the little/junior Mama).

Mankessim Market - Located in the western region of Ghana. Man(township) kessim(big). Literally translated as 'a large township'. This is a popular market in Ghana.

Medasi - 'Thank you' in the Fanti language.

Mekaw Maaba - 'I am going, and I will return' in the Fanti language.

Minerals - Ghanaians refer to soft drinks, e.g. sodas as minerals

Mirikoda - English translation: 'I am going to bed'.

Mirinda - An orange flavored soft drink.

Nkrumah Museum - A museum commemorating Kwame Nkrumah Ghana's first head of state. It is located opposite the parliament house (the old polo grounds).

Obeisance - Some Ghanaians show respect to family members who are highly thought of. Such tributes may be referred to as obeisance.

Obonin - Among the Ashanti people, obonin is the name used for barren women.

Obruni - When used generally refers to Europeans.

Okrawa - Among the Ashanti people, okrawa is the name used for childless men.

Okomfo Anoyke - The name given to Kwame Frimpong. It means the priest who does wonders. From the Golden Stool legend, Okomfo Anoyke is the person who summoned the golden stool, which united the Ashanti people, from the heavens.

Old Polo Grounds - Located across the street from the parliament house. This is where Kwame Nkrumah gave his Ghana independence speech which ended in 'Ghana is free forever'.

Onipanua - Onipa(human) nua(sibling) Translates 'my fellow human being'. Onipanua was the name of a hospital ship working on the Volta River.

Osagefo - The name given to Kwame Nkrumah. It means 'freedom fighter'.

Osu - A well to do section of Accra. The Christiansborg Castle (similar to the white house) and the DuBois Museum are both there.

Otumfuo - A title used with Asantehene. It translates to 'Almighty'.

Plantain - A starchy food in the banana family that has to be cooked. It is popular in the Caribbean and West Africa.

Sankofa - An Akan proverb which literally means 'return and fetch it'.

Sika gua Kofi - Is the name given to the golden stool. Sika means gold and gua Kofi on Friday (the day the stool was summoned from the heavens) according to the legend of the golden stool.

Talking Drums - Among the Akan, there are said to be drummers who can communicate with each other via the drums. Communication often had to do with death, war cries, or happy events.

Tema - A Ghana seaport town on the Gulf of Guinea east of Accra. It was to be an industrial center staffed by foreign countries for an agreed upon time when Ghana would gain control.

Tesano - Was once an undeveloped suburb of Accra. The excellence of the Atchimota Secondary School seemed to spark development in that area.

Tiger Nuts - Are tasty tubers that grow on the ground like potatoes. Some Ghanaians think that they are an aphrodisiac.

Tribal Marks - Cuts carved, at a young age, into people from some tribes. Tribal marks give information about the person's tribe. The practice was discouraged when Nkrumah was head of state. It is less common today in a manner similar to female circumcision.

Twi - The language spoken by the Ashanti people.

Volta River - The river on which the Akosombo Dam was constructed. It is Ghana's largest river.

West African Historical Museum - A formal name given to the Cape Coast Castle/Dungeon.

Printed in the United States
By Bookmasters